ethical space

The International Journal of Communication Ethics

Publishing Office
Abramis Academic,
ASK House, Northgate Avenue,
Bury St. Edmunds, Suffolk, IP32
6BB, UK
Tel: +44 (0)1284 700321
Fax: +44 (0)1284 717889
Email: info@abramis.co.uk
Web: www.abramis.co.uk

Copyright
All rights reserved. No part of this publication may be reproduced in any material form (including photocopying or storing it in any medium by electronic means, and whether or not transiently or incidentally to some other use of this publication) without the written permission of the copyright owner, except in accordance with the provisions of the Copyright, Designs and Patents Act 1988, or under terms of a licence issued by the Copyright Licensing Agency Ltd, 33-34, Alfred Place, London WC1E 7DP, UK. Applications for the copyright owner's permission to reproduce part of this publication should be addressed to the publishers.

Back issues
Back issues are available from the Publishers at the above editorial address.

© 2009 Institute of Communication Ethics & Abramis Academic

ISSN 1742-0105
ISBN 978-1-84549-397-4

Printed in the UK.

Aims and scope

Communication ethics is a discipline that supports communication practitioners by offering tools and analyses for the understanding of ethical issues. Moreover, the speed of change in the dynamic information environment presents new challenges, especially for communication practitioners.

Ethics used to be a specialist subject situated within schools of philosophy. Today it is viewed as a language and systematic thought process available to everyone. It encompasses issues of care and trust, social responsibility and environmental concern and identifies the values necessary to balance the demands of performance today with responsibilities tomorrow.

For busy professionals, CE is a powerful learning and teaching approach that encourages analysis and engagement with many constituencies, enhancing relationships through open-thinking. It can be used to improve organization performance as well as to protect individual well-being.

Submissions

Papers should be submitted to the Editor via email. Full details on submission – along with detailed notes for authors – are available online in PDF format:
www.communication-ethics.net

Subscription Information

Each volume contains 4 issues, issued quarterly. Enquiries regarding subscriptions and orders both in the UK and overseas should be sent to:

Journals Fulfilment Department
Abramis Academic, ASK House, Northgate Avenue, Bury St. Edmunds,
Suffolk IP32 6BB, UK.
Tel: +44 (0)1284 700321, Fax: +44 (0)1284 717889
Email: info@abramis.co.uk

Your usual suscription agency will also be able to take a subscription to *Ethical Space*.

Annual Subscription

Membership of the Institute of Communication Ethics includes a subscription to the journal. Please see the application form on the last page of this issue.
For non-members:

Institutional subscription	£175.00
Personal subscription	£50.00

Delivery by surface mail. Airmail prices available on request or at the journal's web site.

www.communication-ethics.net

ethical space

The International Journal of Communication Ethics

Contents

Preface   Page 5

1. Introduction

Why did the watchdog fail to bark?   Page 7
John Mair

'In the new digital world, there is a stronger need than ever for   Page 10
subsidised, public-service news'
Robert Peston, BBC's Business Editor

2. The Great Crash of 2008: All signs and no meaning?

Top journos look behind the headlines   Page 23
John Mair

Credit standards deteriorated 'at least in part because of a decline in   Page 25
journalistic standards'
Howard Davies, Director of the London School of Economics

Mea culpa: Why we missed the crisis   Page 28
Brian Caplen, Editor of the Banker

'We were all deluded. That's the long and short of it'   Page 33
Hugh Pym, Chief Economics Correspondent at the BBC

'Far from scaring people, the press were providing readers with reliable   Page 38
information'
Alex Brummer, City Editor of the Daily Mail

Britain's most-read financial journalist calls for more 'caveat reporting' to   Page 42
protect consumers
Martin Lewis in an exclusive interview with John Mair

Why generalists were not equipped to cover the complexities of the crisis   Page 44
Francesco Guerrera, US Finance and Business Editor for the Financial
Times

Five reasons why business journalists were blind to the looming financial   Page 50
crash
Matthew Fraser, former Editor-in-Chief of Canada's National Post

3. The financial PR industry and the Great Crash

Spinning us into trouble? Page 57
John Mair

Shooting the PR messenger: Justifiable homicide or irresponsible escapism? Page 59
Trevor Morris, former CEO of Chime Public Relations

Media manipulation behind the Great Crash of 2008 Page 64
Nicholas Jones, BBC correspondent for 30 years

Disconnection and community: Reflections on public relations in the credit crunch. Page 69
Anne Gregory, Professor of PR, Leeds Metropolitan University

4. So what does it all mean for journalism?

Has the Great Crash seen the end of financial Gung-Ho journalism? Only time will tell Page 75
John Mair

How the US media watchdogs' barking was drowned out by the global asset inflation party Page 77
David Cay Johnston, Pulitzer Prize-winner

When business journalism gets in bed with the financial institutions Page 82
Peter Wilby, media columnist at the Guardian

Why journalists need to relearn the old habits of scepticism, fearless questioning and digging for information Page 87
Jane Fuller, top financial analyst

How blogs challenged and transformed mainstream media coverage of the credit crisis Page 92
Kristine Lowe, media blogger

From amnesia to apocalypse: Reflections on journalism and the credit crunch Page 99
John Tulloch, Professor, University of Lincoln

5. Endpiece

Ethical Space: At the heart of contemporary communication controversies Page 111
Richard Lance Keeble, joint editor

Editorial Board

Joint Editors
Richard Keeble — University of Lincoln
Donald Matheson — University of Canterbury, New Zealand

Reviews Editors
Mary Griffiths — University of Adelaide
John Tulloch — University of Lincoln

Editorial board members
Raphael Alvira — University of Navarra
Dusan Babic — Media plan, Sarajevo
Mona Baker — Manchester University
Porfiro Barroso — Computense University of Madrid & Pontifica University of Salamanca, Madrid
Jay Black — Editor, *Journal of Mass Media Ethics*
Antonio Castillo — University of Western Sydney
Ruth Chadwick — Lancaster University
Saviour Chircop — University of Malta
Clifford Christians — University of Illinois-Urbana, USA
Raphael Cohen–Almagor — University of Hull
Tom Cooper — Emerson College, Boston, MA
Deni Elliott — University of Montana
Chris Frost — Liverpool John Moores University
Anne Gregory — Leeds Metropolitan University
Cees Hamelink — University of Amsterdam
Paul Jackson — Manchester Business School
Mike Jempson — Director, MediaWise Trust
Cheris Kramarae — University of Oregon; Centre for the Study of Women in Society
Takeshi Maezawa — Former Yomiuri ombudsman, scholar/writer
Ian Mayes — Former *Guardian* Readers' Editor
Tessa Mayes — Investigative Journalist
Jolyon Mitchell — University of Edinburgh
Fuad Nahdi — Publisher *Q-news*; Producer Channel 4
Sarah Niblock — Brunel University
Kaarle Nordenstreng — Tampere University
Manuel Parez i Maicas — Universitat Autonoma de Barcelona
Ian Richards — University of South Australia, Adelaide
Simon Rogerson — De Montfort University
Lorna Roth — Concordia University, Montreal
Stephan Russ-Mohl — European Journalism Observatory, Lugano
Karen Sanders — San Pablo University, Madrid
John Strain — Unversity of Surrey
Barbara Thomass — Ruhruniversität Bochum
Terry Threadgold — Centre for Journalism Studies, Cardiff University
Brian Winston — University of Lincoln
James Winter — University of Windsor, Canada

Contact: ICE Administrator, Katherine Hill, Faculty of Media, Business and Marketing,, Leeds Trinity and All Saints, Brownberrie Lane, Horsforth, Leeds, LS18 5HD, UK

Published by: The Institute of Communication Ethics (www.communication-ethics.net) and Abramis Academic (www.abramis.co.uk)

Preface

It is now almost exactly a year since the British (and other) banks got within a whisker of closing their doors and their cash machines stopped dispensing money.

In the autumn of 2008, a Great Crash was closer than we realised. Only now is more truth emerging. A narrow escape but one which came from nowhere for most of the population. Now they are feeling the results in the "real economy" – in their lost jobs, closed businesses/shops and the severe squeeze on their pockets. This crisis will last for years.

This special issue of *Ethical Space* – inspired, in part, from a Media Society/polis@lse event at the LSE which I co-produced with Charlie Beckett in February 2009, would not have been possible without much good goodwill. Goodwill from a stellar cast of writers and goodwill from the publishers, Abramis. Richard Keeble and I thank all who have helped.

We hope this timely collection proves both seminal and thought-provoking. That is why *Ethical Space* exists.

John Mair,
Coventry University and Oxfordshire,
10 September 2009

1. Introduction

John Mair

Why did the watchdog fail to bark?

The recession is here. But, as the Queen so elegantly put it, why did nobody see it coming? If journalists did see it coming, then why did they not report it? That is the theme of this special double issue of *Ethical Space*. Financial journalism has been rampant and supremely confident for two decades and more in the West yet when the wolf came to the door in 2007-8, the watchdog, by and large, failed to bark.

Popular consumer capitalism was unbridled from the ascent of Margaret Thatcher to power in 1979. The City of London became the financial centre of the universe. All human financial life gravitated there. London was calling and calling loudly. Banks became super banks, building societies became banks, new share markets grew up as did a veritable snowstorm of new financial products wholesale and retail. It was a paradise but as it turned out a fool's paradise.

The boom in house prices seemed endless and with no chance of it ever becoming bust. You just had to sit and watch your equity and capital accumulate. It was money for nothing. Likewise in the casino atmosphere of the City of London post Big-Bang fortunes were made or lost on the flick of a trading switch. Paper millionaires appeared overnight. Financiers were the Masters of the new Universe and politicians and journalists were in thrall to them and their magic.

The media industry followed suit. For two decades on both sides of the Atlantic newspapers and TV companies got fatter and more profitable on the back of the finance boom. Quality newspapers such as the *Daily Telegraph* and *The Times* developed special daily supplements to chronicle popular capitalism. Finance journalism became attractive and ambitious young journalists such as Will Lewis (later Editor-in-Chief of the *Telegraph* titles) found their niche there. As the boom in easy credit could not end so neither could the boom in writing about it, could it?

John Mair

Aggressive marketing
Hindsight is too often a good judge. Staid building societies transformed themselves into High Street banks. That meant developing many new products for customers and aggressive marketing. Some, such as Northern Rock, were offering 125 per cent mortgages (so you could furnish the new house in the style to which you wanted to become accustomed) and self certification. You told the bank how much you earned and they lent accordingly. It was a charter for cheats. It could not last. It did not.

The first warning signs came from the USA in 2007 where banks found that those given sub-prime mortgages (in plainer English, down market people who had never thought of ownership and probably could not afford it) were defaulting in droves. That was over there. But soon it came over here as it became apparent to what extent all the world markets were interlinked, mainly through wholesale borrowing and lending, and would rise or fall together. Sub-prime was no longer an American problem alone. It was worldwide. Weasel words such as credit crunch soon became crash!

In Britain, the straw that broke the credit camel's back was the run on Northern Rock on 14 September 2007. This was predicted (or caused? you take your pick) by the iconoclastic journalist Robert Peston on the BBC Network News the night before. This, the first run on a British bank for more than 100 years, with snakes of depositors queuing round the block to take out their savings proved a reality check. It signalled the end of the good times. Northern Rock was saved by the government. For six months they tried to find a private buyer before effectively nationalising it on 22 February 2008. That was a portent of things to come.

Nirvana for socialist idealists
The nirvana of socialist idealists for years – nationalising the banks – was on the way to being expensively realised. Other retail banks – the Royal Bank of Scotland and Halifax Bank of Scotland – found their loan books going very toxic too and had to be saved later that year by public money. Lots of it. So too at least two building societies – Bradford and Bingley and the Dunfermline. The British housing market, the bedrock of so many paper fortunes for the ordinary and not so ordinary man and woman, simply went into freefall. The good times were over.

Protection schemes for investors' savings had to be bolstered by the government as consumers smelt meltdown and shifted funds around. At one point in the autumn of 2008, it appeared the whole world banking system was on the precipice ready to fall into the void of mass failure. One entire country – Iceland – and its banking system whose products had been heavily ramped up by

British journalists, all but closed down at some great cost to British investors. Lehman Brothers, an old and trusted name in investment banking, was allowed to go to the wall by the US government on 15 September 2008.

That proved salutary. Markets crashed and the US administration then decided it had to rescue other big name Wall Street banks such as Goldman Sachs and Citicorp to stop capitalism itself collapsing. The high priests in the Wall Street citadels of free enterprise were now worshipping at the altar of public subsidy. Times had changed. The Great Crash of 1929 was replaying itself in slow motion 79 years later. Phantoms of the Great Depression were coming back to haunt the modern world. The Owl of Minerva was flying overhead. The Masters of the Universe simply had no guides out of the meltdown maze.

Picking through the rubble

In all of this drama, financial journalism found its way out of the ghetto of City pages and supplements to the news pages. This crisis affected everyone. The "credit crunch" (as it was euphemistically dubbed by journos) was now on every doorstep in the land. The good news had become toxic like the debts. Journalists now had to explain to their readers and viewers how their savings, houses and jobs could be saved. *Mea culpas* and explanations of the mess of potage were few.

This special double issue of *Ethical Space* attempts to pick its way through the rubble of the world economy and asks with the help of practitioners, commentators and academics just what brought about this editorial myopia and was there simply too much playing Footsie with the FTSE?

Robert Peston, the Business Editor of the BBC, proved to be one of the very few prescient, if lonely, journalistic voices in the pre-crash wilderness. Put simply, he spotted the excesses and weaknesses and reported them remorselessly. He was right. In our first chapter, he applies that cogent analysis to the future of journalism after the events of 2008.

Note on Editor

John Mair is associate senior lecturer in journalism and events co-ordinator for CSAD at Coventry University. A graduate of the LSE, Leeds and Sussex Universities, he is a former producer and director for the BBC, ITV and Channel Four where he specialised in making current affairs documentaries. He is the chair emeritus of the LSE Media Group, director of events for the Media Society and a member of the Executive Committee of the Institute of Communication Ethics. He is the co-author (with Asa Briggs) of *Marx in London* (BBC, 1981) and he co-edited with Richard Lance Keeble *Beyond trust* (Arima, 2008).

Robert Peston

'In the new digital world. There is a stronger need than ever for subsidised, public-service news'

In his Richard Dunn Memorial Lecture at the MediaGuardian Edinburgh International Television Festival in August 2009, Robert Peston, the BBC's Business Editor, explained why his blog was now the bedrock of his journalistic output – and asked: "Will the new digital news industry promote or undermine the wide distribution of high quality news, which is so essential to a thriving democracy?"

News journalism is struggling to cope with the combination of a collapse in advertising more serious even than the plunge of the mid-1970s and massive, disruptive technological change. It all feels as significant as anything the industry has experienced since the explosive growth of the great mass market newspapers in the early twentieth century or the creation of the BBC and the establishment of its principles of editorial impartiality.

Now it is probably worth pointing out at this early juncture that what follows are my reflections – albeit the reflections of a not particularly dispassionate observer since journalism has been my life for more than 25 years – rather than some kind of official BBC corporate view.

I will be looking at the future of our industry from the corner I know best, which is business and economics journalism. But what I have to say, I hope, has relevance for all news journalism. I want to make four points.

Why the traditional business model needs to be overhauled
First, this is no ordinary recession – the traditional business model of news providers is being wrecked and needs to be overhauled.
Second, in a globalised, 24/7 digital world, individual news organisations may be less powerful than they were, but stories – and to an extent the journalists who own them – shout louder than ever.

Third, I will argue – from my own experience – that the traditional distinctions between television journalists, radio journalists and print journalists are quite close to being obsolete. This has huge operational implications for all media companies and also for regulation of the industry.

Then I will make the case that the financial crisis we're living through – and the end of an era of what I call financial paternalism – shows that more than ever we need a choice of high-quality news providers which are confident in their ability to explain complex important issues in a clear and accessible way. And I will look at whether we can be certain that the commercial news sector's imminent revolution – in launching subscription or paid-for online news services – will meet that important need of any thriving democracy.

I wrote all this before hearing James Murdoch's passionate call in his MacTaggart Lecture for the dismantling of the BBC and the near total liberalisation of the media. But if there is a thread running through my lecture, it is this. Market-based democracies like ours need two kinds of essential infrastructure: robust financial systems that transmit cash and allocate capital where it will be most useful; and competing independent news groups that distribute impartial information so that people can take control of their lives and rein in the over-mighty. We have just seen the near total collapse of our financial infrastructure, to a large extent because of misguided deregulation of banking; so we have to ask whether there is any rational basis for believing that withdrawing all regulation and subsidy from the news market would be any less costly to our way of life.

This has been no ordinary recession

To state the obvious, and to move outside of the media industry for a moment, this has been no ordinary recession. It has been the worst global economic contraction since the Great Depression of the 1930s. And because the crisis had its origin in a glut of debt in the US, the UK and a few other economies, there are reasons to believe that – for the US and the UK at least – recovery may well be a rather long, drawn-out affair. There is also a significant risk that an insipid recovery could be fairly swiftly followed by another recession.

In the good years, a massive rise in borrowing by households, companies, the public sector and (above all) by banks fuelled an unsustainable boom (from which the media industry was a massive beneficiary) and a bubble in assets, notably housing and commercial property.

Robert Peston   Well the party is well and truly over. That said, there are signs that the recession is ending. However the fundamental problem has not been solved. We *were* living beyond our means and we *are* living beyond our means. We have to reduce our debts, but doing that in a fashion and on a timescale that doesn't tip us back into recession will not be easy.

Now there is one thing that is absolutely fundamental to an assessment of how long the UK remains in a period of low or non-existent growth – and that is all about why lending to businesses is so weak at the moment. If that is because banks remain too weak to lend, then that is more easily rectified – as and when banks accumulate vital capital for lending via a recovery in profits that will come in the next year or two. If however – as happened in Japan – the more fundamental problem is that businesses have become chronically averse to risk and have chosen to pay down debt and to invest less, well that would remove a vital component of any serious economic recovery.

Media groups slashing costs and investment
In the mainstream commercial media industry, many big businesses are conspicuously choosing as their priority a Japanese-style reduction of their excessive debts, by slashing costs and investment. And it is easy to see why. Depending on which segment you look at – television advertising, national newspapers, regional newspapers, display, classified – advertising is down by between 15 per cent and more than 50 per cent. Worse still, many of the media executives to whom I talk don't expect any serious recovery over the coming few years – because for the best part of a decade there has been a partial decoupling between the performance of the economy and advertising revenues. Google's income has gone through the roof. But advertising revenues for traditional TV, newspaper and radio companies have risen more slowly than the economy in the upturn, and have fallen much faster in the down turn.

Newspaper advertising revenues are predicted by Enders to be £3.9bn in 2013 – a staggering 48 per cent or £3.5bn less than in 2007. If that's right – and it is supported by what media executives say to me – newspapers will over five years lose advertising revenues equivalent to the entire annual licence income of the BBC. Which is why they need to find new revenue – and it is why charging for online news will become the norm. Television advertising is expected to suffer a bit less – falling from £3.6bn in 2007 to £2.9bn in 2013 – a loss of £700m of revenue. But – as has been widely noted – the aggregate revenues of ITV, Channel 4 and Five (perhaps £2.7bn) are significantly less than the BBC's and about half that of James Murdoch's British Sky Broadcasting.

On the broadcasting side – if classifying a section of the industry in that way makes sense in this digital world – there are a pair of giants and some minnows with loud voices, strong brands but depleted resources. All of which – to state the obvious – makes the large and protected revenue of the BBC and Sky's monopolistic control of satellite distribution much more contentious than would be the case if the rest of the sector was booming. And, of course, it raises the question to which I will return of whether the BBC is the invaluable defender of impartial, public-service journalism, at a time of a massive squeeze on the resources of commercial news providers, or the monstrous squisher of private sector rivals.

To revert to the wider economic picture for a moment, there are two further relevant points to make. First that if there is a widespread trend of British companies paying down debt, as they did in Japan for a decade from the mid 1990s, then that will make it much harder for any new government to cut public spending next year without tipping the UK back into recession. And it would be unrealistic to expect heavily indebted consumers to pick up where they left off two years ago and spend the UK into a new era of growth. On my own estimates, consumers may seek to reduce their debt relative to income by 30 or 40 per cent. Which has negative implications for all businesses depending on consumer spending – and media companies are among those, par excellence.

How consumers and businesses behave depends on what the great economist Keynes called animal spirits. And, as Bob Schiller and George Akerlof – authors of *Animal spirits: How human psychology drives the economy – and why* – recently pointed out, that was an important insight so disastrously ignored by mainstream economists for 60 years. Most economists took it for granted that participants in a market will always behave rationally – which in view of the recent behaviour of bankers would be funny if it weren't tragic. Much greater account of psychology, of how humans actually behave, must be built into models of the economy and the rules that constrain the activities of banks.

"Too much gloom and doom" in the media

Viewers, listeners and readers believe that the media has an impact on those animal spirits, on their own moods and actions. When the BBC polled them in April, 63 per cent thought there was "too much doom and gloom" in the media. As you would imagine, I would disagree that we have been too gloomy – but, of course, I would acknowledge that news stories can have a significant influence on people's psychology and actions. And that influence has increased very significantly as news has gone digital and global – as the run at Northern Rock may remind us.

Robert Peston	Those queues outside the Rock's branches on Friday 14 September 2007, after I had disclosed that it had requested emergency financial support from the Bank of England, came as a shock to me. But as the Governor of the Bank of England has said, the behaviour of Northern Rock's savers in asking for their money back was rational. Northern Rock made lethal mistakes in both the way it borrowed money and the way it lent – and several days passed before the Chancellor of the Exchequer made an unambiguous statement that depositors would not lose a penny. The incident shows how loud a voice a journalist and a media organisation can have and what a heavy responsibility there is to get the facts and context right.

How the media influences animal spirits – on a global scale

What this story brought home to me was how – in a broadband world – the media influences animal spirits unbelievably quickly and on a global scale. The images of the Northern Rock queues were distributed within seconds all over the world, as stills and as video. They came to symbolise the vulnerability of the banking system. And in a UK context, they raised questions for investors and creditors from Boston, Massachusetts, to the Emirates to Tokyo about the viability of other British banks that had many of the same characteristics as Northern Rock, such as Bradford & Bingley and HBOS. Ultimately those banks too would have to be rescued.

It became even harder for journalists to be narrating bystanders, the chorus, rather than protagonists and participants after the collapse of Lehman Brothers, which created hysteria among even the biggest and most sophisticated financial institutions. Again, when I disclosed that Britain's biggest banks had been told by the government that they needed to raise £50bn of additional capital, which meant in the case of Royal Bank of Scotland and HBOS that they would be semi-nationalised, I was staggered when the share price of RBS fell 40 per cent within minutes on the morning of 7 October 2008. But this fall in the share price – and whatever impact there was on the confidence of the banks' creditors and the urgency with which the Treasury then organised a rescue of the banking system – reflected the painful financial reality. It was plainly in the public interest to disclose the weakness of our banks. And the primary justification – for me – of this kind of story is to democratise information that matters to all our livelihoods, which would otherwise be available simply to a few bankers, hedge funds and government officials. That said, no responsible journalist would fail to acknowledge that it would be wrong to weaken such important financial institutions through an exaggerated account of their vulnerability.

The media did little to challenge the consensus

In general, I would say that the media has had a more distinguished record than governments, central bankers, regulators and bankers in both seeing the risks that were being accumulated in the economy during the boom years and spelling out their implications after the summer of 2007, which is when the credit crunch began. But that would be to argue that the media was myopic while the authorities were blind. And some parts of the media did their bit to pump up the bubble. Newspaper property supplements and television's property shows, for example, illustrate the greatest risk for the media in reporting so many issues, but especially business and finance. How do we have the courage and the insight to go against the mainstream and against powerful vested interests? Let's be under no illusion: the media did too little to challenge the consensus that the world had entered an era of continuous low-inflation growth – or at least not until it was too late.

To be clear, our frailty is not in the loudness of our voices – it is in our determination to probe and to challenge orthodoxy. It may be a cliché to point out that there has been a massive fragmentation of news suppliers between the traditional media outlets and a new digital species – many of them highly specialist – with news you can use on everything from the number of potholes outside your front door, or what's going on for hedge funds, plus blogs, Twitter and so on. But although individual news organisations are probably in general weaker, facing both greater financial pressures and more competition than ever, the power of individual stories – and I suppose of journalists, from time to time – has increased.

When a story takes off on the internet, as they have many times in respect of the credit crunch over the past couple of years, it's a massive worldwide explosion. But it's not just business or economic stories. Think about how TMZ's disclosure of the death of Michael Jackson went from internet scoop to global TV news within minutes – or how the *Daily Telegraph*'s website became the primary source on the biggest political story of the year, the revelations about MPs' abuse of their expenses. Which brings me to the associated changes in the way that hacks like me work.

Hacks have to become total journalists

For men – usually men of a certain age – there was no greater pleasure than watching the Dutch football team of the 1970s playing total football. The point about that Dutch team, but especially the inspirational captain, Johan Cruyff, is that all of them could more or less play in every position. And my argument is that hacks like me increasingly have to become total journalists. When I started in journalism, I wrote one or two stories a week on a clunky mechanical typewriter – it was the last century but it really wasn't that long ago. Now I write up to five or six blogs in a single day, I broadcast on the *Today* programme, the *Ten O'Clock*, as the broadcasting pillars of my output, and also on up to 20 or so other channels and programmes in a single day.

Robert Peston

My strong advice to any young person thinking of becoming a journalist is to acquire all the skills. They should not think of themselves as wanting to be broadcast journalists, or radio journalists or print journalists: increasingly it's all the same thing. What matters is what has always mattered – the facts, the story. The skill for a journalist is unearthing information that matters to people and then communicating it as clearly, accurately – and if possible as entertainingly – as possible.

The blog is the bedrock of my output

For me, the blog is at the core of everything I do, it is the bedrock of my output. The discipline of doing it shapes my thoughts. It disseminates to a wider world the stories and themes that I think matter. But it also spreads the word within the BBC – which is no coincidence, because it started life as an internal email for editors and staff. It gives me unlimited space to publish the kind of detail on an important story that I can't get into a three minute two-way on *Today* or a 2 minute 40 seconds package on the *Ten O'Clock News*.

It connects me to the audience in a very important way. The comments left by readers contain useful insights – and they help me understand what really matters to people. That is not to say that I give them only what they want. I retain an old-fashioned view that in the end the licence fee pays for my putative skills in making judgements about what matters. Most important of all, the blog allows me and the BBC to own a big story and create a community of interested people around it. Sharing information – some of it hugely important, some of it less so – with a big and interested audience delivers that ownership and creates that committed community.

Now, because of my own indifference to how I communicate a story, whether by video, audio or in writing, I regard the competition as the *Telegraph*, *The Times*, the *Financial Times* and so on, just as much as Sky and ITN. And what's more for much of my output the competition is not just from UK-based organisations with UK audiences. The *Wall Street Journal*, CNN, *The New York Times* and the *Washington Post* are competitors too.

People want their news via the most convenient digital medium

Also, it is increasingly clear that much of the audience doesn't care whether they receive their information via the blog, some other internet channel, the TV, newspapers or radio. We did a survey in February of where British people get their information about the economy. 84 per cent still turn to television first, but 53 per cent used the internet, as opposed to 52 per cent who go to a newspaper, and 37 per cent radio. For young people in the ABC1 category, 61 per cent turned first to the internet – although even for this group TV was out in front with 74 per cent. The point is that in national and international news, convergence has in a very fundamental sense already happened for TV, radio and newspapers. We all do video, audio and the written word. Digital is our primary distribution network, even if it is a digital link to the micro-printing site in Southern Spain. We are all in the same market.

Here's an odd thing. Technology, working practices and consumer behaviour are all manifestations of the creation of a seamless digital news marketplace. But that is not how regulators or politicians see the news media – or at least not as manifested in the regulations that apply to the market. So a tricky question is whether the rules restricting cross-media ownership remain fit for a digital world. Are the distinctions those rules draw between television, radio and newsprint companies relevant any longer? Is there industrial logic, for example, to the prohibition of a merger between a Channel 3 franchise and a national newspaper with more than a 20 per cent market share? Are those rules promoting diversity, choice and competition? Or are they preventing a much needed rationalisation of the way that news is provided which is neutral about the digital method of delivery or distribution – video, audio, written – and which would release vital resources for what really matters, the journalism, the investigations, the gathering of information?

That said, I am not arguing that there is overwhelming commercial logic for the merger of a newspaper group with ITN or ITV. In a world where Channel 3 and national newspapers are in dire straits, arguably such a merger would create as many problems as it solves. Two weak companies combined often create one much bigger but still weak company. And, as it happens, I do feel uneasy about the idea of a newspaper giant owning ITN, for example. But my uneasiness may not be rational. Are we sure that such a merger would any longer represent a grave threat to democracy? What I am saying – and there is nothing particularly original in this – is that we need to come up with a robust new way of measuring market share in news, one which properly captures both the rise and rise of Google in the advertising market and also doesn't seek to treat a television viewer, a newspaper reader, an internet user and a radio listener as though they are different customers of different industries. They should perhaps be seen, within the news market at least, simply as consumers of news.

But lest anyone should think I am arguing that choice in news provision no longer matters, I am arguing the opposite. In fact, more than ever we need a choice of providers of high quality, authoritative news. The question is how to ensure there are enough competing groups with the resources to invest in news – because it

The need to empower people to participate fully in democracy

In my area, of financial journalism – but I think this argument can be extended – there is more-than-ever a requirement to fulfil that traditional purpose of serious journalism, to empower people to participate fully in democracy. The reason is that for the past 25 years or so we have seen the slow and lingering death of financial paternalism, partly by design of government policy, partly by accident. There was a time when jobs were for life and a decent income in retirement was guaranteed by a benign employer, with the welfare state rescuing the unlucky or feckless few. Those were the days. Whether it's pensions, or buying a house or acquiring new skills so that we can remain in gainful employment, the onus has been put much more on individuals to make decisions that will determine whether they'll be prosperous or paupers. But are we equipped to make those life-determining decisions?

In that poll of earlier this year, the BBC asked those surveyed whether they were confident of explaining some basic financial concepts to a friend. The best result was for interest rates. But only a quarter of the poll was confident they could explain interest rates to a pal. Some 22 per cent felt they knew what the credit crunch was (I'll bet they were wrong), 20 per cent said they understood inflation, and just 11 per cent said they knew what GDP was. Which makes me a bit depressed, given that I have been explaining this stuff for most of my adult life. But my goodness they have a hunger for information: 41 per cent of our poll said they accessed more news as a result of what was going on in the economy. And never in my wildest dreams did I think that my blog would get more than 700,000 hits in a single day. People are desperate to know more. Out of 208 stories covered by BBC journalism between May 2007 and 2009, news about the state of the British and global economy stood out more than any other for our viewers – the election of Obama was placed only 8th, the start of the Beijing Olympics 16th.

The death of financial paternalism

There has been another manifestation of the death of financial paternalism. We have also learned at great cost – from the worst financial and economic crisis since the 1930s – that we can no longer blindly delegate to a technocratic elite, a financial priesthood, vital decisions about how the global economy operates. We were, for example, wrong to allow a self-selecting international elite to set the rules for how our banks – the bedrock of our economy – are prevented from taking excessive risks. These rules – that conditioned how much banks can lend and to whom – were decided completely outside of the normal democratic decision-making processes by a group of central bankers and regulators, the priesthood, gathered together in Switzerland in what's called the Basel Committee on banking supervision.

This may sound tedious and abstruse but it was those rules which allowed banks from Switzerland to the US to the UK to lend more than was sensible or safe relative to their capital resources. The severity of the global recession is directly related to the chronic misjudgements made by the priesthood. It was the system they designed that took the world to the brink of financial Armageddon last autumn. As a banking editor in a past life, I was a rare breed of journalist who took an interest in what they did. And I have to say that I would like that bit of my life back. Because it is perfectly clear to me that I was wasting my time taking them seriously. They weren't simply rearranging the deckchairs on the Titanic, they were actually steering the Titanic – our financial system – towards the iceberg.

And what worries me is that we are trusting these unelected officials from regulators and the central banks – like the Financial Services Authority and the Bank of England – to take these decisions on our behalf all over again, without any serious popular debate about what kind of banking system we want. Unless media organisations are prepared to tackle these unsexy complicated issues, how on earth are we going foment a national debate, how are people going to have a voice on issues that probably affects their prosperity more than whether the tax rate rises or falls by a few percentage points?

What I am talking about here, as you know, is the importance of public service journalism, about informing and educating the public so that there is democratic participation in big decisions about the future of capitalism. Now at a time when the future of the financial underpinning of the economy is in question, so too is another part of the fabric of our society – the part that transmits not money but the news and information we need to hold powerful institutions to account. And for me, the issue is all about securing the greatest access for the greatest number of people to a diversity of competing high quality news sources.

Commercial news groups to start charging for access

Against this backdrop the certainty that commercial news groups will start charging for online access is relevant. We should be in no doubt about this. Every news organisation – with the exception of the BBC – will start charging very soon for any information that has any proprietary element to it at all. As I explained at the start of this talk, there is no way for these groups to survive unless they can generate this additional income. Against that backdrop, much of what the BBC does – especially the stuff we do online – may look like unfair competition (for the avoidance of doubt, I am not advancing the preposterous notion that the BBC is free). And as someone who worked in the private sector without a break from 1983 to 2006 – and who rather assumes that he will return to the private sector one day – I completely understand why James Murdoch has argued that the BBC's online news service looks like state-subsidised unfair competition. Much of the private sector sees the BBC as crowding out legitimate commercial players. I feel the private sector's pain on all this – although there is a counter argument.

With financial paternalism in its death throes, just as we are being forced to take control of our financial lives as never before, are we sure that a wholly liberalised commercial news market would ensure that everyone has access to the kind of news and financial information they need and deserve? There already appears to be a consensus that in the provision of regional news there has been a massive market failure that will require state intervention and subsidy to rectify. But is that market failure limited to regional news?

Will the new paid-for online model inform and educate on hard issues – financial matters, but also medicine, the environment, education and so on – that matter to us, or will it concentrate on the more sensationalist and titillating bangs for the buck? And even if paid-for online services do endeavour to fill the gap created by the death of financial paternalism, will millions on low incomes be excluded from access to this information? Should we be relaxed if can't pay means can't know?

The apples and pears of social justice
There is a debate here about two kinds of fairness. There is the fairness of ensuring a level playing field for players in a commercial market. And there is the fairness of the distribution of information and knowledge to all who need it, irrespective of their material circumstances. These are two different kinds of fairness. They are apples and pears of social justice. But having just lived through the greatest failure in history to distribute financial resources efficiently and equitably, we certainly shouldn't assume that a commercial digital market in news will distribute information in a way that would support a healthy democracy.

Walter Bagehot – as luck would have it the greatest ever writer on banking – defined democracy as government by discussion. But you can't have a decent chinwag without having the facts. And the big question is whether the incipient structure of our new digital news industry will promote or undermine the healthy discussion that is necessary for democracy to thrive.

Note on Contributor
Robert Peston is the BBC's Business Editor, who has broadcast and published a series of exclusive stories about the global financial crisis and the credit crunch. In 2008, he won the Royal Television Society's awards for Journalist of the Year, Specialist Journalist of the Year and Scoop of the Year, the London Press Club's Business Journalist of the Year Award, the Broadcasting Press Guild's Award for Performer of the Year in a non-acting role and the Wincott Foundation's awards for Broadcaster of the Year and Online Journalist of the Year. The previous year, he won the Royal Television Society's Scoop of the Year award (for his exclusive on Northern Rock seeking emergency financial help from the Bank of England). Peston has published two books, *Brown's Britain* – a biography of the British Prime Minister, Gordon Brown – and *Who Runs Britain?*, his account of who's to blame for the economic mess we find ourselves in.

2. The Great Crash of 2008: All signs and no meaning?

John Mair

Top journos look behind the headlines

The essential and most obvious journalistic question following the Great Crash was: Why did nobody see it coming? It was posed by, of all people, Her Majesty the Queen when opening the new academic building at the London School of Economics on 5 November 2008. It could not have been better put by a professional. It rarely was.

The signs of imminent crisis had been there for a year or longer if you cared to look beyond the spin of the financial pages .The brave few like the BBC's Robert Peston, Gillian Tett, of the *Financial Times*, and Will Hutton, of the *Observer*, were seen as journalistic anoraks and isolates left to analyse the fine data in bank reports and in the capital markets, smelling disaster and trying to sound the alarums. They were in a small minority faced with the sheer cacophony of praise for the new capitalism. The mood music was quite simply against them.

How did such a sophisticated constituency as the financial journalists of Britain and elsewhere have the blinkers put on them for so long? Why could they see (or not see) the signs of doom but yet put no meaning to them? We examine this through the eyes of some practitioners and media analysts in this section.

Let's first look at some of the causes and excuses. Sir Howard Davies, at the epicentre of the City of London for many years at the Bank of England and the FSA and now Director of the London School of Economics, spares nobody – all the institutions are to blame. Hugh Pym, who reported the Great Crash of 2008 night after night for BBC TV News, is penitent. Nearly. We were all deluded, he says. That seems the long and short of it. Blame the media by all means. But blame the millions who benefitted from cheap credit too, not to mention the lenders, he says. Brian Caplen, editor of the *Banker*, the parish newsletter for the British banking community, says he was at first very doubtful about new devices such as securitisations but sunk those doubts. In any case, most finance journalists, he

John Mair argues, failed to predict the crisis because they tended to focus on news events and individual banks rather than macroeconomics. Moreover, according to Caplen, a financial crisis on this scale is a once in a century event, "so you could have lived a whole life predicting it and never seen it".

Or as Evan Davis, the distinguished presenter and financial journalist on the BBC, put it: As a financial journalist you wait years for good stories, then one point three trillion (the amount of taxpayers' pounds spent by the British government in bailing out the British banks) come along in one go!

Alex Brummer, who edits the City pages of the *Daily Mail*, the bible of the house-owning classes, attempts to pick his way Socratically through the ruins of the economy whilst Martin Lewis, who runs moneysavingexpert.com and is the most-read consumer financial journalist in Britain, looks at the effect on those that matter-real people. Francesco Guerrara, of the *Financial Times*, provides a perspective from the high altar of capitalism – New York. And to wrap things up, Matthew Fraser, formerly editor of the *National Post* in Canada, now at the INSEAD business school in Paris, puts the myopia of the media down to ignorance and the poor training of financial journalists.

Howard Davies

Credit standards deteriorated 'at least in part because of a decline in journalistic standards'

Howard Davies chaired a debate on the media and the financial crisis earlier this year at the London School of Economics. In his opening speech, reproduced here, he referred to a major American study which argued that "credit standards deteriorated to disastrous levels at least in part because of a decline in journalistic standards over the same period"

Tonight's event is unusual in that it comes to us by Royal Command. When Her Majesty the Queen opened our new building here at the LSE in November, as part of the tour of the building we organised a short presentation on the financial crisis by one of our professors, showing the initial impact of problems in the sub-prime market, then the losses in the banking system, and then the implications for emerging markets, all summarised on three arresting slides.

At the end of the short explanation, Her Majesty said: "That's awful," which as a summary of the crisis in two words takes some beating. But she then went on to ask: "Why did nobody see it coming?" Of course, encompassed in the word "nobody" are many potential actors. The realm of politicians, central bankers, regulators, banks themselves, ratings agencies and even borrowers have come under the microscope. Now it is the media's turn.

A couple of weeks ago, the Treasury Select Committee had a run at this issue themselves, but much of the focus of the questioning was on the rather narrow issue of whether Robert Peston's BBC reporting helped to precipitate the crisis at Northern Rock. We aim to cover a broader canvas this evening.

Some journalists warned
Of course, some people do not accept the premise that the media did not see the crisis coming. Some witnesses at the committee hearing pointed to warnings in some articles they and others had written. To some extent, they made a fair point. But Lionel Barber, editor of the *Financial Times*, acknowledged that it was hard to say that the imminent crisis was the dominant theme in reporting on

financial markets in 2006/2007. Martin Wolf, probably our most distinguished commentator on the economy, has made a similar point.

And it is not only in the UK that the media failed to pick up the crisis at an early stage. A recent article in the *Columbia Journalism Review* by two award-winning financial journalists made the point that while their colleagues are now queueing up for Pulitzer prizes for their post-mortems on the failures of Lehman Brothers, Bear Stearns and so on the real question is rather different: "Where were the same news organisations while the biggest financial story of their lifetime was being played out nationwide?"

They go on to pin quite a significant share of the blame on their media colleagues. They argue that "credit standards deteriorated to disastrous levels at least in part because of a decline in journalistic standards over the same period". This may be a rather grand claim to make, but they go on to suggest some reasons why the media were late in understanding what was going on.

Among the reasons they adduce are: the diminished resources available to many newsrooms at a time of cutbacks in the print media faced with declining revenues, risk aversion on the part of journalists unwilling to challenge the prevailing orthodoxy, a lack of editorial vision. Editors were disinclined to commission or support contrarian investigative journalism; there was a lack of technical expertise among financial journalists, and also of historical perspective. Many had grown up through a period of rapidly expanding financial markets, impaired objectivity faced with "larger than life" heroes such as Alan Greenspan, who was given a very easy ride through most of his time at the Federal Reserve (1987 to 2006).

Excessive concentration on the equity markets
On this side of the Atlantic some of those who gave evidence to the Treasury Select Committee also speculated on why reporting had not been clear enough on the way the crisis evolved. Alan Rusbridger, editor of the *Guardian*, pointed to the excessive concentration on the equity markets, when the problems were really to be found in the debt markets. Robert Peston, of the BBC, has made a similar point, and also points to the extraordinary complexity of much financial market trading, and the difficulty of explaining the nature of complex instruments to a broader public.

Simon Jenkins, columnist on the *Guardian*, *Sunday Times* and *Evening Standard*, argued that journalists had become too close to the City and, therefore, lacked objectivity. They were too credulous about the abilities and achievements of financial market stars. This, in part, might be attributable to the rise of financial public relations – a point made in Damian Tambini's Polis research paper on financial journalism. It may be that all of these explanations have some force. Tonight we will try to tease them out, and see if our panel can produce a more comprehensive response to the question.

Note on Contributor
Howard Davies is Director of the London School of Economics. He was previously Chairman of the Financial Services Authority, Deputy Governor of the Bank of England, Director General of the CBI and Controller of the Audit Commission.

Brian Caplen

Mea culpa: Why we missed the crisis

Brian Caplen, Editor of the *Banker*, traces the origins of the financial crisis to "securitisation" and suggests that most finance journalists failed to predict the crisis because they tend to focus on news events and individual banks rather than macroeconomics

One of the bogeymen of the financial crisis was a previously obscure, but latterly highly damaging, concept known as securitisation. I clearly remember the first time securitisation was explained to me back in the 1990s and the kind of questions I raised.

Basically in securitisation the mortgage the bank gave you on your house (or the credit card debt or car loan) is taken off the bank's balance sheet and put into a made-up company that exists only to receive your mortgage along with thousands of other mortgages. You carry on paying your mortgage every month but instead of going to the bank the money goes instead to the made up company to repay bondholders who bought the mortgages from the bank.

Isn't it a bit of cheek, I remember asking the banker who was explaining all this to me, to take my mortgage and give it to someone else? And what happens if I stop paying my mortgage and the bondholders don't get their money back? I was assured that I would never notice that my mortgage had gone into outer space or more accurately the mid-Atlantic as it turned out – and that so far no securitisation vehicle had ever crashed.

There were all kinds of other technical issues surrounding securitisation such as interest rate risk, the different classes of bonds involved and who would get paid out first in the event of difficulties, collateralisation, sampling procedures and default histories. In the first articles I wrote about securitisation, learned professors spoke at length about these risks and we created quite a stir about the efficacy of this newfangled concept.

Moving on to the next innovation...
But as every journalist knows, a story doesn't remain hot for very long. Soon I had stopped worrying about the intricacies and frailties

of securitisation and had moved on to the next innovation. My colleagues in the financial press no doubt did likewise and the mainstream press hardly ever touched such an arcane subject. Meanwhile securitisation grew into this massive and unchecked industry. Not only were mortgages, credit cards, car loans and the rest being securitised but so too were the flows from a whole mixture of loans jumbled up together. These were called collateralised debt obligations.

Banks were also selling the credit risk of some of their loans by paying a fee to the taker who then became responsible for paying up if the borrower defaulted. Known as credit default swaps, it was this kind of arrangement that proved so disastrous for the US insurance company AIG. Again, I remember asking some, hopefully, of the right questions about this kind of arrangement at the time. For example, if a company got into trouble, how would this affect the bankruptcy process since the banks having sold the credit risk would not care if the company failed? Why were banks making loans in the first place, if they only either wanted to sell them on or sell the credit risk? Why were other banks and insurance companies buying the risk?

Bankers are good at defending their inventions and most of the answers were based on either the theory of comparative advantage – Bank A has access to a particular type of credit risk on terms that Bank B doesn't so Bank B wants to buy the exposure – or the theory of market efficiency according to which the more that risk is sliced, diced and parcelled out to the party that most wants it, the safer and more efficient the total system will be.

Market approach too glib
Like most journalists I recorded the debate and moved on. Little purpose is served editorially in harping on about an impending disaster that fails subsequently to materialise. And these past years have been lonely times for those of us schooled in Keynesian ideas and who always felt that a pure market approach was too glib, too limiting and just too theoretical to correctly explain what was going on. Time and again I've sat through speeches at multilateral meetings where bankers and politicians alike proclaimed that the market had all the answers. These have been the ruling ideas for nearly three decades and they have gone unchallenged because, for so much of that time, their proponents could claim that they were working well, delivering wealth across borders and who were you, insolent scribe, to question their veracity?

Politicians, it's worth saying, of all colours bought into the concept of financial markets always delivering as much as anyone else, and they had a great interest in this outcome in terms of tax revenues from bank profits and jobs in the City. All this made it much more

Brian Caplen

difficult for critics and regulators to be heard even if someone had been persistently calling the end of the party (and there were a few). Officials of the Bank of England expressed their reservations and European Central Bank President Jean Claude Trichet was particularly outspoken on the incorrect pricing of risk, just before the onset of the crisis. All these thoughts and comments were faithfully recorded by journals such as the *Banker* but no action was taken.

The Icelandic case is particularly instructive. Iceland was being described in the press as a hedge fund, not a country way, before it crashed and at the *Banker* we invited all the bankers and leading officials to a roundtable to discuss the country's apparently risk-adverse financial sector way back in June 2006. Councils who held their money in Icelandic banks claiming not to have known the risks just were not reading the financial press.

I think what fooled journalists, regulators, politicians, risk managers more than anything about the crisis, however, was the impact these new instruments and structures could have when they were built up and leveraged on a mass scale. Some of us did write articles about the build-up of leverage but mostly it was considered a matter for individual banks. Few of us spotted how markets were mushrooming and the financial sector as a whole was becoming wildly out of proportion to the real economy it was supposed to be serving.

Speculative to the point of the absurd
Credit derivatives at one stage became a $60 trillion market, about twice the size of world gross domestic product (GDP), which seems speculative to the point of the absurd (although actually, despite all the worries, it seems that in the end most of the contracts settled). Banks were leveraging up their capital 30 times, banking assets had expanded to three and four times the GDP of even relatively large countries like the UK, banking stocks as a percentage of total stock market capitalisation were accounting for a larger proportion than every other industry with shareholders expecting, and long used to, above average returns. Most of us missed all this because we tend to focus on news events and individual banks rather than macroeconomics which doesn't tend to make much of a story.

Massive liquidity was being pumped into the markets as a result of the build up of Chinese foreign exchange reserves. These were being used to make huge purchases of US treasuries (and still are), crowding out other buyers and bringing down yields. There was a desperate search for yield. A prophetic book by Charles Dumas and Diana Choyleva, entitled *The bill from the China shop: How Asia's savings glut threatens the world economy* (Profile Books), appeared as far back as 2006 and was reviewed by the *Banker* as an interesting idea.

That liquidity had to go somewhere and its usual destination, over the 20 years I have been writing about financial markets, were the emerging markets countries with high political risk and weak policies. This time, however, the liquidity wave found the emerging market within the United States: the sub-prime borrower. Again, the warning sign was the massive growth in a market that by definition should have been a minority sport and ancillary to the mainstream. But cracks in the sub-prime market did not go unreported.

In fact, the crisis in the US sub-prime market must surely count as the most well-predicted downturn on record. Journalists and analysts were writing about the likely problems a year or 18 months ahead of its unravelling. But, again, what was missed was the scale of some banks' involvement. They were also using a structuring method that on paper should not have been risky but turned out to be calamitous.

Suddenly we arrive back to all those basic questions about securitisation that were asked a decade ago and subsequently forgotten. No-one was keeping an eye on the quality of assets being put into these securitisations that were being originated by third party brokers in the US. The brokers did not care whether borrowers could repay as they were handing the asset on. To save money the big banks putting together the securitisations had reduced the number of individual mortgages they looked at to assess their robustness. And the rating agencies who were making huge profits out of rating securitisations had no historical default rates to assist them in their verdicts. They chose to artificially construct them.

Sorry to sound like a parrot but if you flip back through your old *Banker* magazines you will find an article written by a credit analyst taking apart rating agency methodology for rating sub-prime securitisations. In the interests of balance and fairness, we also invited a rating agency to reply and defend its position. It makes for a rather technical read and no doubt even some of our readers sighed and moved on to articles with a bit more pace and colour (such as "Team of the month").

Bankers not unduly concerned
The bankers were not unduly concerned because their million dollar risk management systems said that everything was fine. Many of them were borrowing huge amounts of money in the markets and then investing it in the triple A tranches – the highest rated and safest part of the securitisations – to gain a slight yield pick-up. They were not invested in the lower quality bonds or the equity and their risk management systems told them that markets would

Brian Caplen

have to go through an unheard of number of standard deviations for them to ever come unstuck. Clearly it was impossible.

So guess what? That's exactly what the market did do and suddenly securitisations were collapsing left, right and centre and, in a turning of the concept on its head, coming back onto the balance sheets of the banks that originally put them together to take them off balance sheet. This was not supposed to happen but sometimes the banks did this in a desperate bid to salvage their already battered reputations. All this most of us in the financial press did miss, but then a financial crisis on this scale is a once in a century event, so you could have lived a whole life predicting it and never seeing it.

Now politicians and regulators are busy trying to put in place systems to prevent the next crisis. Some of their ideas seem quite half-baked but even if they weren't I guarantee that everyone will miss the next crisis too – due around the year 3000. We all know now about securitisation and its pitfalls. But the next crisis is not going to involve securitisation or bonuses or mark-to-mark accounting or poor corporate governance procedures. By definition the next crisis is going to occur in a shape or form that no-one has thought of and regardless of whatever regulations are put in place.

Need for regulators with political clout

Remember that banks, by their very nature as profit maximising institutions, will always attempt to get round the regulations anyway. Securitisation, after all, was a way of expanding a bank's assets without providing the additional capital that regulators would have insisted on if they had been left on balance sheet. The only salvation is to have regulators who are savvy enough and have sufficient political clout to insist on different responses according to particular problems. Some countries such as Canada, Australia and Spain did have such far-sighted regulators who managed to save their national systems.

But expecting humble scribes to put all these complex concepts together, as well as name the day and form in which the whole thing will all come tumbling down – and run a decade-long campaign for regulatory change and oversight – is probably asking a bit too much.

Note on Contributor

Brian Caplen has been Editor of the *Banker* (www.thebanker.com) since 2003. He joined the Financial Times Group from *Euromoney* in 2000 where he had been executive editor for five years. He also worked as a business editor and journalist in Hong Kong and the Middle East for ten years. He has travelled extensively and done numerous high-level interviews with prime ministers, finance ministers, central bank governors and senior executives. He has a first class honours degree in Development Studies from the University of East Anglia.

Hugh Pym

'We were all deluded. That's the long and short of it'

Hugh Pym, Chief Economics Correspondent at the BBC, says just about everyone is responsible for the credit crunch. So blame the media by all means, he says. "But blame the millions who benefited from cheap credit too, not to mention the lenders. And don't forget the governments who basked in the apparently eternal sunshine of robust economic growth and low interest rates"

The Queen, no less, posed the key question on a visit to the London School of Economics (LSE) late last year. Why, she asked, had nobody predicted the credit crunch? There must have been some awkward shuffling as the cream of the nation's economists tried to come up with straightforward answers.

Now, half a year on, Her Majesty has been sent a letter with some explanations. Tim Besley, a member of the Bank of England's monetary policy committee, as well as a professor at the LSE, signed the letter with the political historian Peter Hennessy on behalf of their academic colleagues. They talked of the psychology of denial and concluded that there was "principally a failure of the collective imagination of many bright people, both in this country and internationally, to understand the risks to the system as a whole".

The letter is, in effect, holding all of us to blame. Most economists failed to see the recession coming and then underestimated the scale of it. But they are correct if they are suggesting that bankers, regulators, politicians and the media were found wanting. Journalists should have asked more questions. But so too should MPs and consumers as well as financial market players.

If only the late J.K. Galbraith was still with us. Penguin rushed out a reprint of his classic, *The Great Crash, 1929*. Writing about Wall Street in 1970, Galbraith describes how people had forgotten the lessons of 1929, fuelling another stock market boom and bust: "There is merit in keeping alive the memory of those days. For it is neither public regulation nor the improving moral tone of corporate promoters, brokers…bankers, and mutual fund managers which prevents these recurrent outbreaks…It is the recollection of how, on some past occasion, illusion replaced reality and people got rimmed."

So, it seems, we all forgot previous market crashes and assumed the boom of the early 21st Century was different. Collective wisdom, signed up to by a broad consensus of politicians and media, was that markets would ensure beneficial outcomes. The lightest of light touch regulation was all that was required. Mistaken views were adopted but in good faith. It is worth looking again at the global market developments which preceded the crash.

Public appetite for home ownership grew and grew
As the banks burgeoned after the 1990s recession, the public appetite for home ownership grew and grew. For bankers this was a market which was too good to miss. Mrs Thatcher's government in the UK had encouraged people to fulfil their dreams of owning the roof over their heads. Sales of council houses to tenants became a trademark policy of her early years in power. This policy was supported by Labour after their election victory in 1997. The new government set out their own targets for expanding the percentage of homeowners relative to the total population.

Home ownership became part of the American dream too. Significant political support for expanding property ownership evolved in Congress. But to a much greater extent than in the UK, there was a drive to bring millions of people who had never been in a position to afford a mortgage into the housing market. These customers were known in the delicate jargon of the lending industry as "sub-prime". Wherever they lived, in trailer parks or rented apartments, and whatever their credit histories, they were ripe to be sold mortgages.

While American politicians demanded more housing market funding, a new source of cheap finance for the developed economies was on tap. The Chinese economic miracle was throwing off cash at an astonishing rate. The Chinese authorities pegged their currency to the dollar at a conveniently low rate, so their exports swept all before them in North American and European markets. With exports running so far ahead of imports, China ran up huge trade surpluses and more piles of dollars than they knew what to do with. The Chinese authorities looked to reinvest that cash in overseas markets.

Other Asian economies had also piled up savings mountains and needed to disperse them. But local consumers had been scarred by the economic crises of the late 1990s and were reluctant to borrow their cash. Awash with funding, the Asian banks looked further afield for opportunities to lend it.

Lenders were falling over themselves to find willing borrowers. If the supply of money is outpacing demand, its price will fall. So interest rates came down. At the same time, the Asian tigers, tapping their huge pools of cheap labour, churned out cheap goods such as clothing and electronics for Western markets. Low cost imports, flooding into the developed economies, gave consumers unprecedented bargains. And they proved to be an extraordinarily benign influence on inflation.

Risk of major downturn after dotcom bubble burst

Policymakers at the time were focused on the risks of a major downturn after the bursting of the dotcom bubble. Share prices had tumbled as the internet boom unravelled. Then after 9/11 fears of a slump in the world economy intensified. The United States experienced a short recession. Alan Greenspan, chairman of the US central bank, the Federal Reserve, slashed interest rates to try to keep the economy ticking over in the face of a downturn. His actions were followed in varying degree by other central banks, including the Bank of England.

And so the intriguing cocktail of financial elements which would fuel a lending binge and surge in property prices was shaken up and stirred. Cheap money – and plenty of it – swilled around. Inflation and interest rates were both low, which meant that in real (that is, inflation adjusted) terms the cost of borrowing was low.

As banks sought out new lending opportunities, investors became obsessed with finding higher returns. They wanted more than the low interest rates prevailing in the money markets. To use the jargon, there was a "hunt for yield". They were ready to push a tidal wave of funding at anyone who wanted to borrow. And if more money is available to borrow, more people will be empowered to buy assets such as houses. So demand for those assets and hence prices can be expected to rise.

Banks and mortgage lenders, encouraged by American politicians, pumped increasing amounts of funding into the housing market. The most fertile new territory was sub-prime. In effect, a new market was opening up and there were potentially rich pickings for those lenders who moved in aggressively. Here were borrowers who, because they were deemed to be more risky, could be charged mortgage rates at a chunky premium to rates prevailing in the mainstream mortgage market. The "yield hunters" charged down this path.

Housing market boom

In the ensuing housing market boom, lenders failed to take account of the nature of the risk they were taking on. With property prices apparently rising inexorably, the consequences of default seemed bearable. If a home had to be repossessed it could easily be sold on by the lender. So the higher interest rates charged to sub-prime customers looked like money for old rope.

These more aggressive forms of lending sparked innovations. The traditional retail banking model had seen banks and building societies lend only what they had taken in from savers. Profit came from the predictable, safe and rather dull margin between what borrowers paid and what savers received in interest. But with lower interest rates, persuading new savers to open accounts became harder. New sources of financial liquidity were required. The wholesale money markets offered a well for new finance. Banks could drop their buckets into these markets and then lend it on to homeowners.

The Bank of England estimated that in 2001 British banks were lending roughly the same amount they were taking in deposits. But by the first half of 2008, the surplus of lending over deposits had reached £700 billion. That surplus was funded largely from overseas borrowing by the banks. Nobody predicted that this source of funding would dry up almost overnight. But it did, with Northern Rock the first high profile victim.

Lending and borrowing bonanza
For the years leading up to the summer of 2007 all these factors created a lending and borrowing bonanza. With so much funding swirling around the markets, a surge in property and other prices was the inevitable consequence. Sure enough, a bubble was inflated and house prices climbed relentlessly. The US housing market led the way, with Britain, Spain and Ireland not far behind. In all four countries the average house price rose by 200 per cent or more between the mid 1990s and 2007. Some observers claimed that the price rises were closely related to underlying factors such as the shortage of housing supply, but this was tenuous. In reality, the market had cut far adrift from fundamentals.

Generally at the time all seemed set fair. Not many Cassandras could be heard arguing that the reckless behaviour of the banks would inevitably bring doom. There had been some warnings, including one from the Bank for International Settlements, about the dangerous pricing of the mortgage-linked securities. But the debt-fuelled economies seemed set to continue on their upward trajectory. Most banks found themselves unable to refrain from issuing ever more loans, for fear of missing out on a continued boom, As Chuck Prince, the Citigroup boss, told the *Financial Times*: "As long as the music is playing, you've got to get up and dance. We're still dancing." Mr Prince later fell on his sword, one of the first high profile bankers to quit when the credit crisis struck.

We were all deluded. That seems the long and short of it. Blame the media by all means. But blame the millions who benefited from cheap credit too, not to mention the lenders. And don't forget the governments who basked in the apparently eternal sunshine of robust economic growth and low interest rates.

Note on Contributor
Hugh Pym is the BBC's Chief Economics Correspondent. He is also the author (with Nick Kochan) of *What happened? And other questions about the credit crunch* (Old Street Publishing, London, 2008)

Alex Brummer

'Far from scaring people, the press were providing readers with reliable information'

Alex Brummer, top Fleet Street City Editor, answers some leading questions about the crisis. He argues that, generally speaking, financial journalists are sceptics – and have served the public well

What has been the role of the press in the current economic crisis?

The press has been a critical source of information to all stakeholders throughout the current financial crisis. It has been able to:

- alert the public to potential problems in the banking system;
- keep them well informed about developments;
- explain the rights of the public to deposit insurance and the impact on their mortgages and other loans;
- explain the sources of the problems and analyse their impact on the economy, the world of finance, politics and the future direction of regulation.

It would have been almost impossible to cover an event of this magnitude without some headlines which would be regarded as sensational. Generally speaking the press has sought a reassuring tone. In an age of 24/7 television, events can be exaggerated. The retail run on Northern Rock can be largely explained by technical factors. It was not the BBC Business Editor Robert Peston's fault that the website had shut down, because Northern Rock systems had failed. Nor was it the TV cameras' fault that because Northern Rock had only a relatively few branches with narrow staffing that queues started to form. To blame the media would be a mistake.

As Bank of England Governor Mervyn King has said, depositors, especially those with more than £35,000 (then the limit), were acting in "a rational way". Far more important it would turn out was not the retail run, which we could see, but the wholesale run in which banks in the money markets declined to roll over billions of pounds of loans. They knew what the retail depositors didn't, which was that half of Northern Rock's mortgage book would roll over in 2008-2009. The press, in reporting the retail run, was only giving retail depositors the same information.

Far from scaring people, the press were providing people with reliable information. At the *Daily Mail*, we had to employ a temporary person to assist with the volume of telephone calls. The number of letters and emails rose exponentially. Readers were looking for independent advice and the *Mail* certainly was one of the first places to call. After the dramatic events of the autumn of 2008 and the collapse of Lehman's, few people including the government seemed to recognise the correlation between cutting off the supply of money to the economy and the recession which came very quickly in the final quarter of 2008 and the first quarter of 2009.

The press was widely accused of talking the country into cautious behaviour and recession. No doubt there was something of what economists call a "negative feedback loop". Should reporters have desisted from reporting the endless bad economic data produced by the Office of National Statistics, the Organisation for Economic Coordination and Development, International Monetary Fund and so on? I somehow think not. It may have been that the BBC's relentless charts pointing downwards did make an impact. But they were reporting the facts – a catastrophic decline in production.

Should financial journalists operate under any form of reporting restrictions during market turbulence?

Placing restrictions on the freedom of the press during market turmoil would be counter productive. It is the moment when readers are looking for information on what has happened and analysis of why it happened and explanations about what they should do. Newspapers are also part of the price formation process. They are a vital ingredient in the complex decision process which decides whether shares should be bought or sold. Why would you have an RNS system – regulatory announcements structure – required by the Financial Services Authority (FSA) and others for transparency purposes and only let the professionals have access? That would put other stakeholders from trades unions to consumers and private shareholders at a big disadvantage. There would also be technical difficulties in an age of electronic media.

If respectable newspapers were barred from reporting on events, the information from less well informed sources, without access to senior officials, documents and so, would almost certainly leak out on to web sites and blogs. We see this with all manner of stories. On newspaper finance pages there is at least a formal editing process, whereby the copy goes through several hands, before publication. It would be irresponsible to block reporting during a crisis. Certainly stories could be better sourced, but the rule at the *Daily Mail* is

Alex Brummer that we need at least two reliable sources and a response from the institution concerned before going into print. We also exercise self-restraint. We had a potentially damaging story on Northern Rock in the early part of 2008 when the government was trying to sell the bank. But in response to appeals from the company and an explanation at the highest level from the Treasury we desisted.

Do financial journalists have sufficient expertise in financial issues?

Most journalists would struggle with synthetic CDs and other ridiculous toxic bank concoctions. But the journalist's job is to report what happens. Many of the stories of the last year have been driven by share price falls. Stocks don't just fall, there is always good reason and we have done our best to establish why that has happened. Sometimes there is an effort to blind us with science.

If there is a problem it could be the mismatch of the bullying financial public relations industry – with its various tools and the support of a legal system behind it – against a single journalist pursuing a legitimate inquiry. The amount of dissembling which has gone on through the crisis would have to be seen to be believed. But in almost every case the press has been right to be highly sceptical.

There is room for improvement. I am fortunate: I have a solid economic and financial background, but more importantly more than 30 years of financial journalism behind me. I reported on the secondary banking crisis of 1974-1975 and played a part in investigating London and County Securities. So I have seen it before and have the judgement. But it might help if there was better refresher training for journalists. My preference would be that this was done through City University, London, but there may also be a case for short secondments to the Bank of England (BoE), the FSA and bank dealing rooms. At present only the BoE offers this opportunity which my colleagues have found most valuable.

One weakness in financial reporting of the crisis is that there is a tendency in the national media to focus on cash markets because derivatives and other markets are so impenetrable. It is a credit to the *Financial Times* that it did report on these more *recherché* areas. But it is also interesting to note that even the City's "house paper" – as it is known elsewhere on Fleet Street – buried much of this material among the share prices at the back of the book. Much of the reporting was in technical language which ordinary members of the public would have found as accessible as nuclear physics.

Did the financial media alert the authorities to issues of public concern?

The financial media have always been at the forefront of exposing wrongdoing of companies. Some of the greatest financial scandals of our time from London and County Securities in 1973-74 through the Maxwell scandals (1992-1996) have been uncovered as a result of journalistic inquiry. I first wrote about Northern Rock's securitisation model and my doubts about it in 2002-2003. If only the FSA had paid more attention. I have little doubt that the old Bank of England, with its extensive market intelligence network, would have done. Such tip-offs are invaluable. Resources of newspapers have become more stretched, so those investigatory opportunities are less.

Earlier this year the Serious Fraud Office made arrests in Spain over an AIM company, on London's junior market, which had gone wrong – Langbar. Much of the preliminary investigation of this was done by a colleague of mine, Brian O'Connor, since retired from journalism and now a fund manager. Similarly, we did valuable work on Independent Insurance which caught the eyes of the authorities. The whole issue of directors' pay and remuneration has been the result of journalists hammering away at fat cat awards and payments which are unacceptable. The code of corporate governance grew out of criticism of such practices. The *Guardian's* work on tax avoidance in 2009 exposed the shortcoming of Her Majesty's Revenue and Customs – an issue which I am sure will be pursued by government and regulators. In July, this paper was party responsible for triggering a new tax amnesty programme.

So what can we conclude?
Financial journalism has its faults like all parts of the press. But as a whole it does a good job in checking the wrongdoing of the City. During the peak of the economic boom there was a tendency towards believing that the top financiers such as disgraced Royal Bank of Scotland chief executive Sir Fred Goodwin walked on water. I may have been part of that cult too at times. But generally speaking, like theatre critics looking a new production, we attempt to find the weak spots in company and government announcements. It can be an unfair contest: tough, well paid PRs against young financial writers. But generally speaking financial journalists are sceptics and this has been a great protection for the public.

Note on Contributor
Alex Brummer has been City Editor of the *Daily Mail* for the last ten years. He was previously Assistant Editor, Financial Editor, Foreign Editor, Washington Bureau Chief and Economics Correspondent of the *Guardian* in a career spanning 25 years. He has won numerous journalism prizes for economic and financial reporting, commentary and as a foreign correspondent. He is author of *The crunch* (Random House Business, 2008, updated in paperback 2009). He is the author of several other books including biographies of the businessmen Lord Hanson and Lord Weinstock, both published in the 1990s. He is currently working on a book on Britain's pensions crisis.

Martin Lewis

Britain's most-read financial journalist calls for more 'caveat reporting' to protect consumers

The "TV property porn merchants" come under severe criticism from award-winning financial journalist, Martin Lewis, in this exclusive interview with John Mair

Broadcaster and print journalist Martin Lewis's website (at www.moneysavingexpert.com) is an internet phenomenon with eight million users a month while his email newsletter goes to 3.5 million people. He writes a column each week in the News of the World, and has others in the Telegraph and more than 30 regional papers. He is never off television presenting – from GMTV to Tonight with Trevor McDonald. He won the London Press Club Consumer Journalist of the Year award for 2009.

When Lewis starts a campaign – such as his long-running one on repayment of bank charges – financial institutions tremble. Lewis has the ear and can feel the pulse of the financial product-buying masses. A recent survey placed him second as the choice for People's Chancellor behind Sir Alan Sugar and a long way ahead of the politicians. Last year, an authoritative study listed him as the most-searched person on the web in the latter part of 2008, beating US President Barack Obama by 11 per cent.

Lewis, who has been covering financial products for well over a decade, categorises himself as a consumer finance journalist and is scathing about the recruitment process for some younger journalists. He says while at the top end the knowledge levels are great, for some, the personal finance or business is a section they fall into as they can not get into news. There's no passion for it and many can't read a balance sheet nor create a spreadsheet, he says.

Losing trust in the banks
What has hurt his constituency most is not the markets' crash but the day-to-day recession-based consequences of getting a mortgage and keeping a job. They lost their trust in the banks during the Great Panic of 2008 when there appeared to be dangers of bank

collapse. But as a result many have learned to spread savings to minimise exposure and he believes the worry over safe savings has dropped, evidenced by page impressions on his safe savings guides dropping from the millions to the mere 100,000s.

His ire is reserved for some of the financial PR industry who presented bare faced lies about the safety of British and foreign banks within weeks of their crashes. Yet he says part of the problem is not the over-influence of financial journalism but its under-coverage. While in these times of crisis it's easy to get front page reports on finance, during the boom, those preaching balanced views found it hard.

But his prime ire is saved for what he dubs the "TV property porn merchants": those television property shows presented by pundits whose job it was to ramp up prices. Writing as far back as 2006, he warned that the powerful presence of these shows meant people thought renting a dirty word, and that they should borrow every penny possible to get on the housing ladder. In the end it would often lead people into misery. But it was these TV pundits – not his colleagues in the personal finance media with their more conservative views – who received the coverage.

Lewis says the financial consumer is starting to realise they shouldn't trust the banks. The campaign for reclaiming bank charges has shown that banks can and will act unlawfully, and in their own interest – not that of the consumers. This, coupled with increasing debt-averse feelings, may be one of the benefits of the credit crunch. Perhaps a less trusting public will make better decisions.

Telling people to save money
He says the only change in his work since the credit crunch is to include more explanations about worse-case scenarios. In all other ways it's the same game: continuing to tell people to save money. Yet he says that journalists need to be more robust in explaining that in some areas there is no such thing as certainty, and the public needs to accept sometimes there are no right or wrong answers.

Anyone who tells you house prices will definitely rise or fall is lying, he says firmly. We need the public to understand that on such risk-based concepts even the experts don't know the answer. Simply: more caveats are needed in journalism.

Francesco Guerrera

Why generalists were not equipped to cover the complexities of the crisis

Francesco Guerrera, US Finance and Business Editor of the *Financial Times*, argues that journalists were lied to by many who were benefiting from the boom. But they were not good enough to see through the lies

Late September 2008 was a miserable time in New York. Memories of the hot, sticky summer were already beginning to fade and the hint of chill in the air was an unwelcome harbinger of yet another of the city's frigid winters. The weather's declining fortunes added to the sense of foreboding and fatigue that permeated the *Financial Times*' newsroom in midtown Manhattan.

We were just coming off the most extraordinary set of events many of us will ever get to report on: the collapse of Lehman Brothers, one of Wall Street's oldest investment banks, and AIG, the world's largest insurer, the subsequent paralysis in global financial market, emergency actions by central bankers across the world and widespread panic among investors.

As the excitement generated by those heady autumn days had begun to subside, my colleagues and I were feeling a little burnt-out and had begun expressing a wish rarely heard from daily newspaper journalists: we were longing for a period of "normalcy", a "quiet time". But the financial crisis was not going to let us off the hook that easily.

The rumblings of the next big story had begun shortly after the Lehman drama: a big retail bank in the US was about to fail. After weeks of reporting and looking at share price movements, we had enough to run with a story: we knew the name of the bank (Washington Mutual, the sixth-largest bank in the US at the time), the reason for its deep-seated problems (sub-prime mortgages) and we had even heard that frightened savers had begun taking their money out.

But neither the *FT* nor rival media organisations dared raising the prospect of a WaMu collapse in the run-up to its failure – which duly occurred on 26 September when regulators seized it and sold off some of its parts to JPMorgan Chase. We did reports on its plunging share price and increasingly-doomed efforts to shore up liquidity but never mentioned the possibility that, within days, WaMu could be no more.

Self-censorship over WaMu's distress
It was self-censorship, at least at the *FT*. We discussed it internally and concluded that by splashing the prospect of WaMu's distress on the front page, we would have provoked a run on the bank and killed off its last, desperate, attempts to survive. Was that a responsible attitude or a reprehensible failure to get an important story out?

The question, in different guises, has been hurled at financial media ever since the financial crisis exploded nearly two years ago. From media experts, to academics, bloggers, and even dinner party guests, the charge has been the press failed to forewarn the public a huge bubble was about to burst and, to a lesser extent, that it was slow and sloppy in covering it once the crisis erupted.

This point of view was summarised by Will Hutton, the former editor of the *Observer*, when he said: "General journalists, as well as business journalists, are really guilty in this. They have indulged madness in the last five years."

I beg to differ, at least with regards to the corner of the press that I know best: printed media (I have different views on how television, especially in the US, handled the turmoil but that is really not my area of expertise). It is true: the press was far from blameless in its coverage of both the pre-crisis and the crisis itself. Unlike WaMu, where we knew but did not tell, there were issues which even experienced financial journalists knew little about.

This was no 1929 stock market crash, when blue-chip, household names saw their shares fall to zero in a matter of hours. The current malaise found its roots in hidden corners of the financial world: not many reporters working for mainstream publications had heard of collaterised debt obligations and auction rate securities but it was those, and other, complex and under-reported instruments which became the epicenter of the financial earthquake that shook the world economy to its foundations.

The criticism that the media was looking in the wrong places for evidence of cracks in the world financial order is also well-founded. I myself wrote extensively on how the excessive debt loaded by private equity groups on the companies they bought before the crisis would prove their undoing. I was only half right: over-leverage was one of the key reasons for the turmoil but among banks and consumers, not private equity.

Don't blame the media
But blaming the media for failing to spot a crisis that was missed, by their own admission, by monetary authorities, credit rating agencies, economists and the world's top bankers (and this is not an exhaustive list), is too facile a knee-jerk reaction. Let me address some of the specific criticism in detail.

A common accusation is that mass media failed to spot the crisis because they were afraid of upsetting their advertisers – the large corporations, banks, and, crucially, property developers that were making billions of dollars by inflating the bubble. Danny Schechter (2009) provides a relatively cool-headed summary of this line of attack in the *British Journalism Review*. In the words of Mr Schechter, an American blogger, investigative journalist and film-maker: "The newspaper industry became, in some communities, the marketing arm of the real-estate industry. In some cities you actually had newspapers getting a piece of the action of sales through the ads they generated – they were actually part of the corruption."

This crisis is, in many ways, a story of conflict of interests (banks' profits depended on their ability to produce ever-complex securities they could sell to investors, credit rating agencies were paid by banks to rate the securities they themselves produced and investors had powerful incentives not to ask questions to lock in favourable returns).

But it is difficult to see how media outlets could have been gagged by their advertisers. Even leaving aside the strict separation ("Church and State" we call it at the *FT*) between editorial and commercial sides that is respected in most English and US publications, the mechanics of the crisis, and the way journalism works, argue against it.

For Mr Schechter's thesis to be right, there should have been a concerted effort by powerful corporate interest to ban coverage of the "property miracle" experienced by the US and many European countries – one that we now know was based on the ridiculous notion that house prices would never decline.

In reality, the opposite happened. Property groups, banks and even corporations fed off the housing bull market and could not have not been happier advertising, and giving interviews about, how they were profiting from the boom and how the new age of prosperity was sustainable.

Similarly, the idea that advertisers could stifle investigative work by journalists on these matters is simply naïve. Long-term investigative projects are rarely (never?) known to advertisers and vice versa: reporters tend to know, or care, little about who advertises in their outlet. Short of postulating that a cadre of corrupt editors *around the world* "leaked" plans for investigative articles to Big Business – a stretch even for conspiracy-theory-friendly bloggers – it is hard to see how such corporate censorship could have taken place.

Reality not flattering for the profession

My fear is that the reality was a lot simpler – but still not very flattering for our profession. The reason why there was a dearth of investigative work before the crisis is that for decades that genre of journalism has been in decline. The dire financial straits much of the media finds itself in meant that the fourth estate was unprepared and underfunded to spot the coming turmoil.

A variation of Mr Schechter's corruption criticism maintains that journalists and editors had become captive of the people and companies they were reporting on. Bruce Watson, of the US finance news website DailyFinance, went as far as talking of an "institutionalised Stockholm syndrome". "Much of the financial media have been all too easily swayed by the arguments of the very people and institutions they were supposed to watch," he wrote in an article on 28 May.

Mr Watson is on to something. Journalists have to strike a delicate, and ultimately imperfect, balance between keeping their sources sweet, maintaining access to corporations and their executive officers, and unearthing stories that both contacts and companies might not like. But in most cases, this stops well short of a "Stockholm syndrome". The incentives journalists have to get ahead in their profession make sure of that. Let's face it: every reporter wants to be on the front page (or in the lead slot in the evening news) and the best way to do that, at least in financial journalism, is to get scoops on "sexy stories": wrongdoing, scandals and other assorted malfeasance (remember the old US television news adage: "If it bleeds it leads"?).

While access is important, indeed crucial, to getting to the right story, self-interest dictates that, when faced with upsetting a source or a company or landing a major story, a journalist would opt for the latter and live with the consequence of the former.

"Trust me, I am a journalist"

In making this argument, I do realise I am asking readers to take a leap of faith ("Trust-me, I am a journalist") into believing reporters will not succumb to the vested interests of their sources. And I am not saying such a thing cannot happen. All I want to add to the discussion is that my experience in journalism – especially in scoop-getting journalism – suggests otherwise.

What I think happened during the crisis is that journalism's traditional tenet of presenting two sides of the same story backfired. When the media did find evidence of problems in the housing market, in financial derivatives or even in the business models of banks (as many of us did and wrote about), it had to give the subject of their stories the right of reply, and to faithfully report what they said.

What those subjects did say, to paraphrase, was: "Nothing to see here, move on." I have notebooks laden with complacent quotes from bankers, regulators and "experts", challenging/deriding the notion the US housing bubble would burst, or even acknowledging it was a bubble.

How could I and others not report that? Had we ignored such claims – and the enormous profits and skyrocketing share prices of the companies that benefited from the boom – we would have been accused, as we have many times during less turbulent times, of needless scaremongering, of crying wolf where there was nothing but sheep.

We were lied to. We were not good enough or resourceful enough to see through the lies. But we were lied to by a whole set of people with a vested interest in prolonging the boom. So if there is a charge that should stick to our brethren at the end of this crisis, it is not the one of corruption, or being enamoured of our sources. If anything, we should be accused of incompetence and ignorance. We did not know and we did not do enough to find out.

As the *FT*'s editor Lionel Barber wrote in the newspaper on 22 April, financial journalists failed to grasp the consequences of a wave of deregulation that followed the end of the dotcom bubble, did not understand the risk posed by the giant US mortgage financiers Fannie Mae and Freddie Mac, and did not dig deep enough into the trillions of dollars in assets banks parked outside their balance sheets to minimise regulatory scrutiny.

Decline in numbers of specialist reporters
And that is partly due to the way the profession has changed over the years. Aside from the decline in investigative firepower mentioned above, the financial strictures of many publications meant that fewer and fewer media outlets can afford specialist reporters. The trend has been towards using journalists as "heat-seeking missiles" generalists who can be deployed wherever the news agenda goes. The downside was that neither they nor their editors were adequately equipped to deal with the complexities of this crisis, especially when it came to predicting it.

Having dealt with the many shortcomings by the mainstream press throughout this article, I would like to conclude with a provocative question to the so-called "new media" – the blogs, internet sites and even television channels that have set themselves up as an alternative to traditional outlets.

My question is simply: where were you? If, as many of you correctly say, "Big Media" did a bad job of predicting the crisis, what stopped you from filling the gap? I have my ideas but that, as Michael Ende said in the *Neverending Story*, "is another story and shall be told another time".

Reference
Schechter, Danny (2009) Credit crisis: how did we miss it? *British Journalism Review*, Vol. 20, No. 1 pp 19-26

Note on Contributor
Francesco Guerrera is the US Finance and Business Editor for the *Financial Times*. His beat includes US financial services and large US-based corporations including Citigroup, JP Morgan and General Electric. Guerrera joined the *FT* in 2000. Before his most recent appointment in 2008, he served as the *FT*'s US Business Editor during 2006-2007, where his beat included corporations, investors and capital markets, and before that he was the Asia financial correspondent, based in Hong Kong. There, he covered merger and acquisitions activity, in addition to regional business and financial affairs. Before his Asia post, he was based in Brussels reporting in the European Union competition, financial services and internal market matters. Prior to joining the *FT*, Guerrera was on the City and Business desk of the *Independent* and covered financial news at AFXNews. He earned a first-class degree in Economics and Journalism from City University, London, and speaks fluent Italian, Spanish and French.

Matthew Fraser

Five reasons why business journalists were blind to the looming financial crash

Matthew Fraser explores the structural dynamics of business journalism to answer the question: Why did the media get it so wrong?

In the painful aftermath of a financial crash, it's easy to identify the culprits. The financial meltdown of 2008 was no different. But as Bernard Madoff and others guilty of less monumental defalcations face the prospect of lengthy incarceration, there remains a more intriguing question: why did so many market insiders in our modern global economy fail to see it coming?

That includes the media. Business journalists have escaped the general opprobrium towards docile regulators and winner-takes-all players on Wall Street and in the City. But some are now asking why so many business journalists did not comprehend – and, more importantly, failed to report – the enormity of the problems unfolding before their eyes as they covered the markets.

In politics, the press is considered a "fourth estate" – part of a system of checks and balances – that scrutinises the actions of governments. Yet in the arcane precincts of banking and stock markets, this high-minded duty is often neglected as business journalists get swept up in the irrational exuberance that drives markets upwards towards their inevitable collapse. What does this failure tell us about the ethics of business journalism?

Andrew Palmer, banking correspondent of the *Economist*, laid most of the blame at the door of regulators and banks but acknowledged that business journalists were not paying sufficient attention. "At the time when these risks were building, when banks were writing cheap credit, when we were all getting drunk on debt, no one was actually asking really difficult questions systematically about the dangers that that posed," he noted after the collapse.

Many business journalists diligently covered the daily dramas as large banks such as Northern Rock began to falter. But the overheated climate of excess was not just a series of individual events. There was a big picture that was largely overlooked. Howard Kurtz, who covers the media for the *Washington Post* and hosts a programme on CNN, wrote in his newspaper column: "The shaky house of financial cards that has come tumbling down was erected largely in public view: over-extended investment banks, risky practices by Fannie Mae and Freddie Mac, exotic mortgage instruments that became part of a shadow banking system. But while these were conveyed in incremental stories – and a few whistle-blowing columns – the business press never conveyed a real sense of alarm until institutions began to collapse."

True, a few astute business columnists had been warning about ballooning credit markets long before the crisis hit. But most business journalists behaved like everybody else in a financial bubble, reacting when it was already too late. As Howard Kurtz noted, the business press was "a day late and several dollars short".

Structural dynamics of business journalism: The pressure for scoops

So what went wrong? The answer lies in the structural dynamics of business journalism and the status attributes to which professional journalists aspire. Five traits can be highlighted:

First, business reporting is driven by competitive pressure for scoops. This leaves little time for off-diary features, analysis and "big picture" reflections on larger trends. Richard Lambert, director-general of the Confederation of British Industry, raised this issue in a speech in late 2008 when he observed that the advent of round-the-clock digital channels had created an aggressive scoop-driven ethos that frequently leads to sloppy reporting. Lambert, a former *Financial Times* editor, contrasted this competitive journalistic culture with the cosy relationships between business reporters and bankers in the early 1970s when Britain suffered its last major banking crisis.

The fact that those tacit codes spared financial institutions the panic of aggressive press scrutiny does not seem to justify nostalgia. More to the point, even if Lambert is right, the fact is that the new culture of aggressive business journalism failed to dig and get scoops on the coming economic collapse. The scoops came only after the crash had happened.

Lack of professional training in business

Second, journalists lack professional training in business. It is an embarrassing fact, but nonetheless true, that very few top-level business journalists possess professional qualifications – such as MBAs – that could equip them with the quantitative skills needed to grasp the fine-print of the complex dealmaking they cover. Many business journalists are exceptionally bright, but they lack rigorous financial training. Dan Bogler, the *FT*'s managing editor, has acknowledged this problem: "Unfortunately, financial journalists – and the *FT* has better-trained financial journalists than others – don't really understand this stuff, and they join a long list of people that starts with the bank regulators, central bank regulators and money managers."

This problem is more acute in Britain, with its long-established elitist tradition at the quality newspapers and the BBC, which have preferred to hire generalists from Oxbridge. While the American media's "professional" pretensions can be criticised, it finds at least some justification in MA-level training at top journalism schools. The American media are also more pluralistic sociologically, with many reporters coming with degrees in business and law.

Business journalists have short memories

Third, business journalists have short memories. Economists frequently observe that our collective memory of previous financial crises is never sufficient to prevent the recurrence of a similar frenzy. True, the 2008 financial collapse had its own characteristics and was not identical to previous stock market crashes and speculative bubbles. But the underlying cause of these painful episodes is invariably the same: cupidity, and in many cases stupidity.

While it is true that young business journalists today have no memory of the 1987 crash, and much less the UK banking crisis of 1973, most can recall the high-tech bubble a decade ago. But memory is no guarantee that journalists learn more from history than investors. Most business journalists were as short-sighted as everybody else on Wall Street and in the City.

Cheerleaders for speculative frenzy

Fourth, business journalists are cheerleaders for speculative frenzy. Walter Bagehot, the celebrated editor of the *Economist* in the 19th century, observed that "people are most credulous when they are most happy". This undoubtedly explains why over-leveraged homeowners and over-bonused investment bankers were blinded by credulity and greed. It may also explain why so many seasoned business reporters failed to blow the whistle.

The uncomfortable truth is that most business journalists were enjoying the upward spiral as much as the investment bankers and analysts whom they counted among their best contacts and lunch companions. Why spoil the party? Some media outlets even deliberately fuelled the financial frenzy. Jim "Crazy" Cramer, the former Wall Street insider and founder of TheStreet.com, hosts a CNBC show fittingly called *Mad Money*. A bombastic market evangelist, he once predicted that Google shares would hit $1,000 – just before the stock plummeted $400 to hover just above

$300. The host of another CNBC business show, Maria Bartiromo, is affectionately known as "Money Honey", a nickname that seductively evokes the sweet taste of speculative frenzy. The bitter aftermath is another story.

Dangers of rocking the boat
Fifth, business journalists do not rock the boat because their careers may suffer. Courageous, indeed, is the columnist who pens a trenchant opinion piece about pervasive greed and an imminent crash. This lesson has many historical precedents. The most spectacular came in September 1929, when a wealthy US businessman, Roger Babson, wrote: "Sooner or later a crash is coming, and it may be terrific." The press was not listening. *Barron's*, the business magazine, dismissed Mr Babson as a crackpot. Others were less courteous. He was, of course, proved right.

The late economist John Kenneth Galbraith wrote in *A short history of financial euphoria* (1990) about an opinion piece he had submitted to *The New York Times* in 1986 predicting a crash. The newspaper politely declined to publish the article, gently informing him that his dire warnings were "too alarming". The *Atlantic Monthly* did agree to print the article, however. A few months later, when the crash began, business journalists across the world were frantically calling Galbraith, *post facto*, for his expert insights.

During the recent upward spiral, journalistic complicity and self-censorship were compounded by an adulatory cult of the chief executive. When colourful business leaders such as Sir Alan Sugar and Donald Trump become television celebrities with their own shows, you know the marriage of media and money has been consummated.

Even the quality press was in awe of the CEO superstar. Take this 2006 headline in *Fortune* magazine about Lehman Brothers' chief Richard Fuld: "The improbable power broker: how Dick Fuld transformed Lehman from Wall Street also-ran to super-hot machine." Two years later, Fuld oversaw the bank's collapse and extinction. When the markets were hot and bonuses bloated, however, CEOs like Fuld were too often revered as all-powerful and quasi-infallible.

What future for business journalism?
What about the future of business journalism? The good news is that the structural dynamics and status attributes described above are being radically transformed by web-based forms of news-gathering and information dissemination. In the short term – as we are already witnessing throughout the newspaper industry – there will be painful structural adjustments as old media organisations downsize and adapt to new realities. In the long term, this rupture

Matthew Fraser   will be good news as business journalists become more independent from, and less complicit with, the markets they cover.

In the past, as Richard Lambert noted, business journalists and bankers belonged to the same social circles and had relationships based on mutual trust and reciprocal favours. In some cases, financial journalists – such as former *Economist* editor Rupert Pennant-Rea – took senior jobs at grand institutions such as the Bank of England. The two worlds shared more than common values. Established business reporters, like bankers, worked for large, vertically structured corporate bureaucracies. Media companies were, like financial institutions, capitalist corporations. Their substantial resources allowed newspapers and magazines to hire large staffs of reporters to cover markets. Journalism was a business that covered business.

While this is still true, it is rapidly changing as new forms of journalism emerge on the web. The web-based journalism revolution – from blogs and podcasts to self-organised forms of "citizen" journalism – has shattered the vertical dynamics of journalism. The internet has loosened the cosy relationships that structure the culture of tacit complicity between media and money. The basic architecture of networked, web-based information and opinion is not vertical, but horizontal. There are virtually no barriers to entry in the web sphere, where yesterday's "professional" journalists are increasingly challenged by so-called "amateurs" – terms that, in fact, have no meaning because journalism was never, formally speaking, a profession in the first place.

The distinction, in fact, is utterly meaningless. While newspapers have successfully moved online, rival news sites frequently feature experts who know a great deal more about markets than most salaried business reporters or columnists. A good example is Henry Blodget, the former Merrill Lynch analyst who became the poster boy for the high-tech bubble a decade ago. Blodget has since re-emerged as an influential blogger, at BusinessInsider.com, on the media and technology industries.

Blodget, thanks to his professional training and expert knowledge, is a rich source of information and analysis. He regularly scoops the established press with highly accurate information accompanied by granular analysis. The *Atlantic* magazine, in a feature article on T*he New York Times*, noted that Blodget's blog provided the "smartest on-going analysis of the company's travails".

As the web rises, newspapers will sink
There are now Henry Blodgets emerging on the web in virtually every sector. There will be many more as unprofitable, printed newspapers vanish. The web revolution will also have significant

consequences for corporations – including banks – that can no longer cultivate business journalists through clubby relationships and expect predictable behaviour from them. In a world of web-based networked information, companies will find it harder to spin and control the message. The blogosphere is not only instantaneous and global, it knows neither fear nor favour. This explains why big PR agencies are invading the web to commercialise their services. Early experiences, such as corporate blogs managed by PR flaks, show that these strategies often backfire. The blogosphere is quick to shame corporate spinning.

It would be naïve, however, to believe that high-profile bloggers won't succumb to the familiar blandishments and inducements that once co-opted the complicity of newspaper reporters. Web-based business reporting will not be exempt from ethical issues. There can be no doubt, however, that these internet-driven changes will trigger a large-scale shake-out in traditional journalism.

While the web revolution is bad news for printed newspapers in the short term, it may turn out to be unexpectedly good news for business reporting. There will always be a market for reliable information and sharp analysis.

Note on Contributor
Matthew Fraser, a veteran business columnist and former Editor-in-Chief of Canada's *National Post*, is a senior fellow at the INSEAD business school in Paris and adjunct professor at the American University of Paris. He is the author of *Throwing sheep in the boardroom: How online social networking will change your life, work and world* (John Wiley and Sons, 2008).

3. The financial PR industry and the Great Crash

John Mair

Spinning us all into trouble?

Alongside the massive expansion in easy mortgages, credit derivatives, credit swaps, private equity companies in the big and seemingly endless boom before the crash, one industry benefited more than most: financial public relations. It and the boom were like a horse and carriage. Huge companies such as Chime, Brunswick and Dewe Rogerson grew up in the City of London and elsewhere and huge fortunes were made "spinning" the new financial products, promoting them to journalists eager to fill the burgeoning financial sections in their papers.

Financial journalism consumed "product" and stories voraciously. There was much space to fill for an industry and lay readers eager to find out how to continue making "loadsamoney". Sometimes the journalist/PR relationship smacked more of market manipulation with, for example, journalists on Sunday business papers regularly fed morsels in the "Friday night drop" that would affect share prices. It became an institution and one that worked. Prices did often shift before markets opened on Monday mornings.

It mirrored what was happening in politics especially under "New Labour". As you had to read the Sundays' lobby correspondents to find out what the political masters of "spin" were planning to tell the public and parliament the next week (with Tony Blair, Gordon Brown and Peter Mandelson kings of this dark art) so you had to read the Sunday business sections too to find out what might happen in the markets. "Spin" proved transferable between spheres – look at Sir Tim Bell who "span" politically for Prime Minister Margaret Thatcher but also built up a huge business empire on financial spin.

In this special edition of *Ethical Space*, former Chime MD Trevor Morris, now a visiting Professor at the University of Westminster, calls for some mercy and understanding of his former role. Attacking PR for being biased is like saying the sea is wet. It is a statement of the obvious, not a meaningful criticism. Within the confines of the law, the job of a PR practitioner is to promote the interests of their client,

John Mair

he says. On the other hand, the journalist who made it his lifetime's mission to root out and expose "spin" in politics, the BBC's former political correspondent Nicholas Jones, argues here: "Financial and political PR were coupled firmly together on the same track; the overriding priority was the need to defend threatened institutions and shore up the system." It worked until the Great Crash.

Britain's first full-time Professor of PR, Anne Gregory, takes a more detached and moral view in her *tour d'horizon* of the ethics: "Public relations practitioners must be clear about their own moral standards and work to a carefully thought-through and enacted ethical compass that runs like DNA through their thinking and actions" is her *cri de coeur*. How much of that was heeded in the heat of the credit boom is open to some question.

Whatever the "truth", however defined, for the golden decades from 1987 to 2007, the financial PR industry succeeded in "spinning" the rest of the world into a situation that ended in a mess. Capitalism became genuinely popular, possibly for the first time ever, but in that popularity lay the seeds of disaster.

Trevor Morris

Shooting the PR messenger: Justifiable homicide or irresponsible escapism?

Trevor Morris argues that blaming the PR messenger for the banking crisis is as facile as blaming journalists. Moreover, it allows people to avoid asking the really difficult questions about why and how a whole society came close to economic collapse

Speaking at a debate attended by around 450 people and organised by Polis and the Media Society, titled "Why did nobody see it coming?", Alex Brummer, of the *Daily Mail*, said: "The press has found itself up against an unnerving banking PR machine whose job it is to dissemble, lie if you like, to put you off track" (Amos 2009).

He was not alone in this view, although his was the most extreme. Gillian Tett, of the *Financial Times*, described coming "up against the financially powerful City PR lobby, with considerably more resources than my team" and talked of "ferocious" PR companies (see Beckett 2009).

A rather different view was given by Charlie Beckett, director of Polis, in his blog on the debate headed "Don't shoot the messenger: media and the economic crisis" (ibid). Whilst he mentioned the attacks on PR, his main focus was on the responsibility of journalists. But PR wasn't to get off that lightly. Paul Seaman (2009), a PR blogger, retorted to Beckett with: "Should the PR industry make a calibrated apology for its contribution to this recession? I think so." (The phrase "calibrated apology" seems to have been used without irony!)

He continued: "It [the PR industry] cannot hide behind the systemic nature of the crisis anymore than can bankers, politicians and regulators. For our place at the table of recovery an apology is overdue."

So why did the bank PR machines come in for such criticism? I contend that there are three reasons why bank PR – and much other PR too – is so often attacked. The first reason revolves around PR's trouble with the truth. The second around journalists' antipathy towards PR people and the third is the tendency for both proponents and critics of PR to grossly over-claim for its power and effectiveness. But before we look at the reasons for the attacks on PR we need to examine what PR actually is.

In our book, *PR – A persuasive industry: Spin, public relations and the making of the modern media* (with Simon Goldsworthy, Palgrave Macmillan 2008) we define PR as "the planned persuasion of people to behave in ways that further its sponsor's objectives. It works primarily through the use of media relations and other forms of third party endorsement" (102). PR thus defined can be and is used on behalf of not just banks but also NGOs, charities, churches, governments and celebrities. Whether or not you think PR is good or bad seems to depend very much on its message and whether or not you trust the messenger.

PR and the truth
It is certainly not uncommon for the PR messenger to come under attack. One of the most common uses of the term PR is as a pejorative: PR stunts, PR job, PR spin and so forth. If we like an attempt to persuade people we call it "a campaign". If we don't much like it we call it "PR" and if we hate it we call it "propaganda". Both sides in any debate invariably decry the other side's communication as propaganda. They seem to be saying: "We are honest, ethical and truthful; the other side is not."

The problem for PR is that truth is a slippery concept and is hijacked as often by the pious, pompous and self-righteous as it is by the outright dishonest. Journalists like to believe they are in search of the truth whilst the trade bodies of the PR industry claim they are committed to telling it (see International Public Relations Association 2009). But often the so-called truth is simply a point of view supported by a highly selective group of facts.

The reality is that PR people seldom lie or at least seldom tell big "black is white" sorts of lies. This is because, apart from the ultimate sanctions imposed on them by regulators and the laws of fraud and libel, PR people and their clients know only too well that the media generally has the last word. There is simply no evidence that before the recent financial crisis the PR departments of banks wittingly lied or set out to deceive the media – if they had why was the media unable to prove it, expose them, and thereby create a powerful news story? Similarly there is no evidence that the competing "PR machines" conspired to outwit or deceive the media. Apart from anything else any one of the banks would have gained enormous competitive advantage by outing their alleged co-conspirators, rather as Virgin outed BA over price fixing.

In reality, what seems most likely is that the banks believed their own PR – as did governments, regulators and to some degree the media. However, what the bank PR machines did singularly and collectively (in the latter case through their trade associations) was to present their clients in the most positive and optimistic light. But this sort of bias is hardly surprising. Attacking PR for being biased is like saying the sea is wet. It is a statement of the obvious, not meaningful criticism. Within the confines of the law the job of a PR practitioner is to promote the interests of their client. Inevitably, the interests of a client sometimes do not coincide with the interests of other groups in society – groups which more often than not have their own PR teams representing their point of view.

Indeed, many would argue – and I am one of them – that with less time and resources for investigative journalism it is an increasingly important job of the media to evaluate and arbitrate between the competing claims of PR operators in the market place of ideas, beliefs and products. As Evan Davis, of the BBC, remarked at the Polis debate, it is "the job of journalists to withstand the pressure of the public relations industry" (Amos op cit).

However, there was in the banking crisis a lack of alternative PR from critical and well-informed pressure groups and think tanks. The media often relies on these sorts of bodies for an alternative view. For example, it is unusual for a corporate body to make an environmental claim without a journalist checking with an NGO to identify their take on the issue. In the absence of this sort of PR balance it was much easier for the PR of the banks to go largely unchallenged. Ironically, in the banking crisis it may have been the case that there was not too much PR but not enough.

Journalists' attitudes to PR
Undoubtedly journalists are increasingly dependent on PR for alternative points of view, information and even story ideas. Perhaps one of the most significant reasons why journalists have been so keen to criticise and sometimes blame PR people is that as the time and resources available to them to research stories has declined their dependence on PR people has increased.

For his 2008 book, *Flat earth news*, the *Guardian* investigative journalist Nick Davies commissioned research from Cardiff University about the sources of UK news stories in Britain's five most prestigious newspapers. The research found that 60 per cent of the stories comprised wholly or mainly PR material and/or wire (news agency) copy, and a further 20 per cent contained clear elements of PR and/or wire copy (Davies 2008: 52).

Davies also found that average staffing levels were slightly lower than twenty years before, but the amounts of editorial space they were required to fill had trebled (ibid: 63) Not surprisingly, given these figures, an increasing amount of what is published in the national media – and in particular in the supplements and other sections designed to attract advertising – is oven ready and even pre-cooked PR rather than original journalism. Davies blames PR for many of journalism's problems, describing it as "the industry that is subverting our news".

Not everyone is so hard on PR. In a speech to the Reform Media Group in December 2008, Richard Lambert, now Director General of the CBI but also in the distant past a "junior bottle washer" on the *Financial Times*'s Lex column, contrasted the banking crisis of 1973-75 with the current banking crisis (Lambert 2008). He observed that with the increase in the interest in business matters following deregulation in the 1980s and the explosion in the number of media outlets: "financial PRs have become central figures in the game…their clients need guidance through a jungle of highly competitive and sometimes hostile news media. And journalists need information that's suitable for their audience, and which comes in timely and readily digestible fashion".

With this rise in the importance of financial PRs and the change in the regulatory and media environment, Lambert noted that journalists now have less exclusive access and fewer "cosy relationships" than in the past and have therefore tended to become more aggressive. However, he also argued: "The old system of business journalism, based on a system of implicit favours between the reporter and the reported, is not to be lamented at all. Competition helps to keep people on their toes, and honest" (ibid).

To support Lambert's point, it would certainly seem naive to imagine that old-style, long lunch briefings between a newspaper's City desk and a banks CEO would have been any more effective at avoiding the crisis. But whilst in theory financial journalists may now be more independent than in the past they now have, as we have observed, less time and resources to capitalise on that independence.

What is certainly true is that there are now more PR people than journalists in both the UK and the US (Davies op cit: 85) and that PR people – particularly in the City – are better paid. But what is also true is that the vast bulk of PR output is unused and that journalists not only have the last word on what is used but on how it is used.

Is the power of PR overrated?
One of the biggest problems for PR is that both its proponents and critics overrate its power. Despite the claims of some in the industry, PR people very seldom play a role in defining the objectives of the organisations they represent. Few PR people sit on boards

and virtually none make it to the very top and become CEOs. Another limiting factor in the power of PR is that few PR people are sufficiently expert to question deeply what they are told by the CEO and experts within their organisation. Like their journalists, PR people cover a wide field of activity from consumer affairs to public affairs and complicated financial deals. They also often move from industry to industry. They simply do not have the knowledge or time to challenge the experts and superiors who brief them – though one would hope they would challenge obvious requests to be dangerously misleading or dishonest.

It is understandable that journalists and others wish to lash out at the banks and their PR departments. However, it is misguided. PR was not responsible for the speculation and lending decisions which brought the financial world to the brink. Blaming the PR messenger for the banking crisis is as facile as blaming journalists. It is an act of escapism that allows people to avoid asking and answering the really difficult questions of why and how a whole society came close to economic collapse.

References

Amos, Owen (2009) Journalists attack City "PR machine" over banking crisis, *Press Gazette*, 24 February. Available online at http://www.pressgazette.co.uk/story.asp?storycode=43161, accessed on 1 May 2009

Beckett, Charlie (2009) Don't shoot the messenger: Media and the economic crisis, Director's blog, 24 February. Available online at www.charliebeckett.org/?p=1133, accessed on 1 May 2009

Davies, Nick (2008) *Flat earth news*, London, Chatto and Windus

International Public Relations Association (2009) IPRA's mission, IPRA.org. Available online at http://www.ipra.org/ detail.asp?articleid=26, accessed on 1 May 2009

Lambert, Richard (2008) Speech at the Reform Media Group dinner. Available online at http://www.cbi.org.uk/pdf/20081205-Richard-Lambert-speech-Reform-Media-Group.pdf, accessed on 1 May 2009

Seaman, Paul (2009) PRs (not journos) should apologise for the crunch, 21st-century PR issues. Available online at http://paulseaman.eu/2009/02/prs-not-journos-should-apologise/, accessed on 1 May 2009

Note on Contributor

Trevor Morris is Visiting Professor in Public Relations at the University of Westminster and co-author with Simon Goldsworthy of *PR: A persuasive industry?* (Palgrave Macmillan 2008). He was formerly CEO of Chime Public Relations, the UK's largest PR group.

Nicholas Jones

Media manipulation behind the Great Crash of 2008

Nicholas Jones, for 30 years a BBC political and industrial correspondent and now a prominent member of the Campaign for Press and Broadcasting Freedom, reveals how the government sought to manipulate the media coverage of the crash. Once again leaks to favoured journalists and briefings to selected news outlets were the order of the day

Not since the hostile take-overs of the mid to late 1980s has there been a sustained focus on news from the City of London which has approached anything like the intensity of the media coverage generated by the Great Crash of 2008. Just as manipulation of the media played a key part in the dramatic bids and mergers of the Thatcher years, so it did twenty years later as Gordon Brown's government struggled month after month to control the agenda and maintain public confidence in the financial system.

Once again leaks to favoured journalists, advance guidance and briefings to selected news outlets were the order of the day. Downing Street and the Treasury were anxious to do all they could to avoid a calamitous run on the banks and a repeat of the devaluation of the pound which followed Black Wednesday and Britain's withdrawal from the Exchange Rate mechanism in 1992. Managing market expectations became the be-all and end-all of the government's communications strategy even if it meant flouting the rules by having to sanction the advance trailing of market sensitive information.

Aiding and abetting the government's efforts to minimise the fallout from alarmist headlines about the credit crunch were some of the City's leading public relations consultants who had in the past been either New Labour sympathisers or apparatchiks. Financial and political PR were coupled firmly together on the same track; the overriding priority was the need to defend threatened institutions and shore up the system.

PR consultants emerge as key players
Public relations consultants first emerged as key players in the City of London in the mid-1980s once the Thatcher reforms began to

bite. The privatisation of nationalised industries, and the sale at knockdown prices of shares in public utilities such as gas, electricity, water and telecoms resulted in a phenomenal increase in the level of personal share ownership. A lighter regulatory regime on take-overs encouraged aggressive bids and unexpected mergers among the household names of British industry and commerce. Business news moved from the City pages to the front page. Newspapers expanded their coverage and began producing separate supplements concentrating not just on what was happening in the City of London but also offering advice on personal finance. Instead of merely reporting the latest share prices, television and radio stations developed separate news sequences and programmes devoted to financial news.

Astute financial PR was regularly a vital factor in clinching hostile take-overs; PR consultants learned how to exploit what had proved to be a significant shift change in the balance of power between journalists and those seeking to manipulate the flow of information from a vast array of public, private and commercial sources. So rapid had been the expansion in the coverage offered by newspapers, television and radio, and so great was the demand for fresh material, there were plenty of opportunities to fine tune sophisticated routines for controlled and co-ordinated leaking.

Tip-offs to financial journalists and timely, off-the-record guidance could help secure positive reporting – or perhaps negative coverage for a rival suitor – which, in turn, might generate the kind of sharp fluctuations in share prices which could transform a company's value and prospects during an unwelcome take-over. Business sections in the Sunday press were a prime target for what came to be known as the "Friday night drop". These newspapers had space to fill and were desperate for exclusive stories which City PR consultants were anxious to place in the hope of influencing opinion over the weekend prior to the start of trading on the Stock Exchange.

Because of repeated allegations about insider trading, rules were introduced to curb leaks about bids and profit warnings and the Financial Services Authority was finally given the power in 2001 to prosecute listed companies which failed to ensure the "full, accurate and timely disclosure" of price sensitive data; in future announcements would have to be made when the stock market was open.

Deliberate leaking of ministerial announcements
No such rules have ever been enforced at Westminster where the pre-announcing of government decisions, although frowned upon by the Speaker, is now considered a fact of life in the cut and thrust of modern politics. While every administration has been anxious

Nicholas Jones to influence day-to-day news reporting, and if possible prepare the public for significant or perhaps unpopular decisions, there has been a step change in the deliberate leaking of ministerial announcements in the hope of gaining favourable coverage.

Perhaps not surprisingly, given the expertise which they had acquired in the 1980s, some sympathetic PR consultants were keen to assist in the rebuilding of the Labour Party under Neil Kinnock. Brian Basham, founder of the City PR consultancy Broad Street Associates, was asked to advise Peter Mandelson, the party's newly-appointed director of communications. When interviewed for my book *Trading information: Leaks, lies and tip-offs* (Politico's, 2006), Basham explained why the competitive pressures building up within the news media meant that political journalists at Westminster were as desperate for scoops as their colleagues on the City desks and why he was convinced the demand for exclusives could be exploited: "I was the one who coached Mandelson. I had to explain to him that news and information had become a currency, which could in effect be traded with journalists in return for sympathetic treatment."

No wonder within months of being installed in Downing Street as Tony Blair's press secretary, Alastair Campbell persuaded the relevant permanent secretaries and succeeded in re-writing the rule book for government information officers instructing them to "grab the agenda" by trailing ministerial announcements. Departmental staff were told to ring round newsrooms to alert journalists as to what to expect. Trailing was in effect deliberate leaking by another name but Campbell argued that in a 24/7 media environment the government had to try to influence the agenda and steer the debate if ministers were to stand any chance of getting their message across to the public.

Gordon Brown – arch exponent in the advance trailing of announcements

During his long years in opposition Gordon Brown had been a regular conduit for publicising confidential documents leaked to him by civil servants and on becoming Chancellor of the Exchequer in 1997 he soon established himself as the government's arch exponent in the advance trailing of announcements. On the strength of his tip-offs he made friends for life among respected financial and political correspondents. In his decade at the Treasury he progressively disregarded all the ballyhoo about pre-Budget purdah and the traditional secrecy surrounding the contents of the Budget box. Each spring and again in the autumn, ahead of the financial statement, Brown would manipulate the build-up, preparing the ground for any changes which he intended to make in tax and spending. By choosing the correspondents to be briefed in advance he hoped to exercise a degree of control over the presentation of his policies and, indeed, so successful did he become in managing expectations that there were rarely any real surprises left when he finally appeared at the despatch box.

During my thirty year stint as a BBC correspondent I observed at first hand how effective selective briefings could be. Key individuals such as the political, economics or business editor would be briefed on a personal basis by Downing Street or the Treasury and advised on the likely direction of forthcoming announcements. BBC newsrooms would then be informed either by an advisory note or by news copy under embargo. Once the story broke news bulletins and programmes across the radio and television output would be aware of the story line. In my experience, when it came to crisis management, government departments rarely took the risk of leaving the BBC out of the loop. Other broadcasters and leading newspapers were more than likely to have been given similar advance warning but the BBC often had the edge because of its ability to deliver a critical audience at key moments in the news cycle and because of the authority of its reporting.

Never having personally achieved editor status I speak largely as an observer and once I started chronicling New Labour's spin routines in articles and books, I found I became only an occasional recipient of critical off-the-record guidance. Nonetheless, the BBC's key role in reporting the ongoing drama surrounding the Great Crash of 2008 followed a pattern which I recognised only too well. The pre-announcing of hurried rescue operations for failed banks and troubled financial institutions seemed to be well co-ordinated and designed to minimise alarm. Late-breaking stories on the *Ten O'Clock News* or early on *Today* provided investors and the City of London with vital reassurance that action was being taken.

Praise for Peston's "personal integrity"

Nothing that I have written seeks to detract in away from the award-winning run of exclusive stories delivered by the BBC's Business Editor Robert Peston. He was in the right job at the right time and, unlike his competitors, he did have unlimited access to the broadcast platforms which mattered most of all to the government. But he still had to rise to the occasion – which he did in his own inimitable style. Peston upheld his personal integrity, demonstrating his news sense, his independence and an air of detachment which only comes with years of experience and the hard-won respect and trust of some extremely well-placed contacts.

As one momentous rescue followed another I was reminded of the cavalier days of the 1980s when the pre-release of price sensitive information had similarly been so commonplace during hostile take-overs. However, such was the turmoil in the markets caused by the credit crunch, and so urgent was the need for financial firefighting, that there was inevitably scant regard for the FSA's rules on market sensitivity and the requirement for "full, accurate and timely disclosure". From what I was able to piece together from talking to other journalists, Downing Street and the Treasury were both reliable sources, assisted on occasion by a number of well-placed PR consultants.

While ministers might seek to defend the institutionalised leaking which occurred on the grounds that the government was in the middle of a financial crisis, an ethical line was crossed quite frequently. My own researches have revealed previous examples of confidential Whitehall media plans which have explicitly referred to the advance trailing of financial announcements on *Today* and in newspapers such as *The Times*. When the taxpayers' interests are at stake, it seems the rules on insider dealing have to take second place.

In the event of a new Conservative government it is likely to be as assiduous as the administrations of Blair and Brown in seeking to manage the presentation of economic policy decisions so as to avoid uncertainty in financial markets. When in July 2009 the Shadow Chancellor George Osborne published his proposals for changing the system of banking regulation and abolishing the Financial Services Authority, he ensured the key announcements had been floated in advance.

Osborne prepared the ground for a Sunday morning interview on the *Andrew Marr Show* by trailing the key points in *The Sunday Times*; when Robert Peston delivered his report on the BBC *Ten O'Clock News*, previewing the launch the following morning, he said he had "here the policy document which will be published tomorrow". If politicians are to be heard amid the clamour of 24/7 media environment they know they have no alternative but to find ways of influencing the news agenda. If needs be, journalists have to be briefed in advance and given an outline of market sensitive information. Despite the bank collapses and associated crises of the Great Crash of 2008, the Treasury did succeed more often than not in guiding the direction of the news coverage, a lesson that will not be lost on any future Conservative chancellor.

Note on Contributor
Nicholas Jones has written extensively on the relationship between politicians and the news media. His books include *Strikes and the media* (1986), *Soundbites and spin doctors* (1995), *Sultans of spin* (1999) and *Trading information: Leaks, lies and tip-offs* (2006). News archive: www.nicholasjones.org.uk

Anne Gregory

Disconnection and community: Reflections on public relations in the credit crunch

Top PR academic Professor Anne Gregory explores the question: How can public relations contribute in the post-credit crunch world?

Introduction
The economic downturn experienced in the last 18 months has brought into sharp focus a number of issues which those with foresight in the public relations profession might have seen as predictors of impending crisis. These issues are as complex as society itself, with many interplaying dynamics and will be deeply contested as hindsight shines a spotlight on recent events.

Themes within three arenas pertinent to the practice of the public relations profession are discussed here briefly. These relate to issues in society, organisations and the profession, and cohere around the notion of disconnection. They seek to answer partially the question: "How can public relations contribute in the post-credit crunch world?"

Society
Claims that the credit crunch heralded the end of free market capitalism abounded in the press in 2008 (e.g. Milne 2008; Wolf 2008) but already there are suggestions that the moment of crisis has passed (Wolf 2009) and that adjustments to, rather than abandonment of the system will suffice. When and at what cost the credit crunch will end is open to debate, but what appears to have more longevity at this juncture is a shift in the public mood. Other concurrent events, such as the further breakdown in trust between the UK electorate and parliament as a result of the expenses scandal precipitated by revelations in the *Daily Telegraph*, have compounded that shift. This has been accompanied by a falling level of trust in business generally. The Edelman Trust Barometer for 2009 (Edelman 2009), in its 10th annual survey of opinion formers, noted a 16 point fall in trust in banks to 31 per cent, with energy dropping 13 points to 32 per cent.

Anne Gregory

In recent research a group of communication directors working for financial companies such as Bear Stearns, Babcock and Brown and Lehman Brothers (Thompson 2009) were astounded by the ferocity of the media onslaught by those with whom they had enjoyed good (the word used by interviewed journalists was "embedded") relationships. Indeed, the print media, under enormous pressure to turn around falling circulation figures, stand accused of cynically exploiting financial and political scandals. According to John Lloyd, formerly of the *Financial Times* (Pitcher 2009), they have transformed into an industry more concerned with the exercise of their own power than the scrutiny of the power of others. According to the Edelman report (Edelman 2009), trust in newspapers has dropped to just 19 per cent.

The credit crunch, then, prompted by a culture of greed and the unbridled activity of free market capitalism, cynicism about the political system and reduced trust in business and the media, has precipitated a significant disconnection by the general public from those philosophies and institutions that have underpinned much of society in the early 21st century. The public sphere is polluted, confused, cynical and looking for new answers.

Organisations
Against this backdrop, organisations and institutions are attempting to stabilise their own reputations and fortunes. However, their steps are sometimes inappropriate and serve to compound the problems, not solve them. For example, there has been some apparent public contrition by financial institutions. The apology to the Treasury Select Committee by the former chief executives and chairmen of HBOS and RBS was meant to serve as a kind of public expiation, but was marred by their apparent tutoring by public relations professionals and the size of their remuneration and severance packages.

Recent news that one of the instruments that led to the financial crisis – namely large city bonuses – are returning, with record payments to staff at Goldman Sachs, Credit Suisse and even RBS which is now 70 per cent owned by the UK taxpayer (Finch 2009; Inman 2009) only serves to exacerbate public cynicism.

More positively, many organisations, sensing the public mood, have responded more in line with public expectations. For example, they have either increased or decided not to cut their Corporate Social Responsibility (CSR) programmes (*PR Week* 2009). Other CEOs have attempted to set an example or to ameliorate the impact of the recession on their workforce by freezing executive pay and offering a range of cost-cutting options to employees rather than making compulsory redundancies, such as extended leave, part-time working and agreed salary cuts (Martindale 2009).

Other organisations, such as the UK supermarket chain ASDA, have taken action to align their activities to the public mood (Willis 2009). Their *Pulse of the nation* research indicated that celebrity lifestyles were dissonant with the realities facing families having to deal with the effects of the recession. Consequently they have ended the link with celebrities such as Colleen McLoughlin (wife of Manchester United and England footballer, Wayne Rooney), who promoted their George fashion brand, and now use "real people" as models because they are seen to add more value.

Despite these initiatives there is suspicion about motives. The most cursory Google search about reduced executive pay, reveals accusation of a "PR stunt". A similar search about CSR reveals that many companies are involved because it makes good business sense. ASDA's initiative could again be seen as a clever move to protect its business.

So what is the public mood on these issues? Research by the Arthur W. Page Society in the USA (Arthur W. Page 2007) before the recession revealed that people are seeking "authenticity". Indeed, their research report is called *The authentic enterprise*. The test of authenticity is lived values and transparency.

The profession
In the light of the foregoing, what responsibilities does the PR profession bear? Doubtless extremely large amounts of money have been earned by those agencies working in the specialist financial and political PR sectors, and extremely large salaries are paid to those who work for large corporate organisations. The reason those people are employed is to promote and defend the organisations by whom they are employed. Some argue that serving the free market is amoral (see Pitcher 2009). An extension of that logic is that to serve your organisation is amoral. The often-drawn parallel is that public relations advocacy is akin to legal advocacy: the case for organisations should be made as powerfully as possible, bought to the court of public opinion and tested. The parallel is, of course, false. There is no judge to ensure that opposing voices are heard in equal measure and to see fair play. There is no "legal support" for those who cannot afford or do not have the knowledge or power to gain access to the court of public opinion. Free-market principles reign here too.

The Code of Conduct for the Chartered Institute of Public Relations (CIPR 2009) states that all members have a duty to have "due regard" to the public interest when undertaking their work. Reports about sharp practice in public relations are legion, but what is rarely covered are the debates that practitioners have with senior managers about defectives which do not take into account the public good. Rarely disclosed, too, are the number of resignations by practitioners who believe their clients or employees are not acting for the public good and who are prepared to go rather than defend those actions publicly.

However, it cannot be disputed that public relations is seen, on the whole, to serve the interests of the large, the powerful, the well-resourced and the self-interested. There is a disconnection between what the professional body espouses and what some members of the profession actually practice, and the dysfunctionality is fanned by an antipathetic media.

Conclusions
So how can public relations contribute to mending the disconnections discussed above? As Pitcher (op cit) says, a new narrative is required which helps to define the public striving for a new articulation of the world and business. In the author's view, the discussion must start in reverse order to the issues presented in this paper. Public relations practitioners must be clear about their own moral standards and work to a carefully thought-through and enacted ethical compass that runs like DNA through their thinking and actions. At a recent gathering of professionals, numbering approximately 100 strong, the author found that only two had undertaken formal ethical training. Ethics begins with choosing whom practitioners work for, whether in-house or in consultancy. Their labour should be given not just according to the size of the reward, but according to the enacted values of the organisation. Does it serve the public good? If not, it does not deserve the support of a professional communicator.

For organisations a deep examination of their values and role in society is required. CSR often comes under the remit of public relations. In the author's view, the phrase "corporate social responsibility" should be expunged from the corporate lexicon. It is too often a convenient box where a series of optional activities are placed to be bragged about when required and dispensed with when the "bottom line" is not served. A responsibility to society, without whose good will and permission organisations would not exist, must be an engrained given. At a deeper level, it is incumbent on public relations practitioners to challenge organisational decisions, acting as the ethical guardian and testing decisions against lived, as opposed to declared values and the increasing requirement of transparency.

At the societal level there is a renewed opportunity for the public relations profession to contribute to what Heath (2008: 96) calls a "fully functioning society". Here practitioners are called on to "embrace Quintillian's (1951) principle of the good person communicating well as a foundation for fostering enlightened choices through dialogue in the public sphere".

The temptation of the industry to serve the highest payers in a free market has to be tempered with the overriding obligation to ensure people are able to make informed choices. The power and attendant responsibility of communication, or public relations, to contribute to this cannot be overestimated. As Williams (1989) asserted, communication and community should be seen as equivalent because communication is central to the creation of society. Through communication, social and individual meanings are formed and by sharing them common ground is found and interpreted.

This higher calling, albeit ideal, must be a clarion call to the public relations industry and aligns with the sentiments expressed by Michael Sandels (2009), the 2009 Reith lecturer, who called for a return to the notion of a "new citizenship" based on the "common good". Kruckeberg and Starck (1998) have encapsulated the concept of common good and community thus:

> A community is achieved when people are aware of and interested in common ends and regulate their activity in view of these ends. Communication plays a vital role as people try to regulate their own activities and to participate in efforts to reach common ends (ibid: 53).

What public relations can help creat is an assertive consensus around this narrative. But, without a reasserted sense of community, however this is defined in the disconnected, geographically dispersed and atomised state in which Western society finds itself as it moves through the credit crunch, there is little hope of discovering a new narrative.

References

Arthur W Page Society (2007) *The authentic enterprise*, New York, Arthur W Page Society

BBC (2009) Former banking bosses say "sorry", BBC News, 10 February. Available online at http://news.bbc.co.uk/1/hi/business/7880292.stm, accessed on 8 July 2009

CIPR (2009) CIPR Code of Conduct. Available online at http://www.cipr.co.uk/membership/conduct/index.htm

Edelman (2009) 2009 *Edelman Trust Barometer*, New York, Edelman

Finch, J. (2009) The new city buzzword: BAB (that's Bonuses are Back), *Guardian*, 24 June. Available online at http://www.guardian.co.uk/business/2009/jun/24/banking-city-bonuses-buzzword, accessed on 8 July 2009

Heath, R. (2006) Onward into more fog: Thoughts on public relations' research directors, *Journal of Public Relations Research*, Vol. 18, No. 2 pp 93-114

Inman, P. (2009) Goldman to make record bonus payment, *Observer*, 21 June

Kruckeberg, D. and Starck, K. (1998) *Public relations and community: A reconstructed theory*, New York, Praeger

Martindale, N. (2009) Redundancy: Top 10 alternatives, *Personnel Today*, February

Milne, S. (2008) Not the death of capitalism, but the birth of a New Order, *Guardian*, 23 October. Available online at http://www.guardian.co.uk/commentisfree/2008/oct/23/creditcrunch-economics, accessed on 8 July 2009

Pitcher, G. (2009) *Mammon, morality and markets*. Presentation to Chartered Institute of Public Relations Fellows, House of Lords, July 2009

PR Week (2009) Marcoms groups throw their weight behind CSR agenda, *PR Week*, 29 May

Sandels, M. (2009) *The Reith lectures 2009*. Available online at http://www.bbc.co.uk/programmes/b00kt7rg, accessed on 14 July 2009

Thompson, G. (2009) *Beyond marketing: Is public relations still strategic?* Paper presented at the Academy of Marketing Conference, Leeds, July

Williams, R. (1989) *Resources of hope*, London, Verso

Willis, P. (2008) *Culture, public relations and the credit crunch: Reflections on the challenges facing practice*. Paper presented at the 16th International Public Research Symposium, Bled, Slovenia, July

Wolf, M. (2008) The rescue of Bear Stearns makes liberalisation's limit, *Financial Times* Economists Forum, 26 March. Available online at http://blogs.ft.com/economistsforum/2008/03/the-rescue-of-bear-stearns-marks-liberalisation%E2%80%99s-limit/, accessed on 8 July 2009

Wolf, M. (2009) This crisis is a moment, but is it a defining one? *Financial Times*, 19 May. Available online at http://www.ft.com/cms/s/0/beb9b7e8-449f-11de-82d6-00144feabdc0.html, accessed on 8 July 2009

Note on Contributor

Anne Gregory is the UK's only full-time Professor of Public Relations and Director of the Centre for Public Relations Studies at Leeds Metropolitan University, which is home to the largest department of public relations in the UK. She is also Pro Vice Chancellor of the University. Before moving into academic life, Anne was a full-time public relations practitioner, holding senior appointments both in-house and in consultancy. She is still involved in practice being a consultant to a number of private sector clients and several UK Government departments. She is an internationally rated scholar and speaker, being published in numerous books and journals and is editor-in-chief of the *Journal of Communication Management* and of the UK Chartered Institute of Public Relations' Public Relations in Practice series of 17 books.

4. So what does it all mean for journalism?

John Mair

Has the Great Crash seen the end of financial Gung-Ho journalism? Only time will tell

The flight into the darkness of recession had little light shed on it by the sentinels of truth. By and large, the Fourth Estate watchdog was found to be a lapdog in the Great Crash of 2008. As the public saw through political spin in Britain and the USA and became increasingly cynical and detached from conventional party politics, so would they lose faith in finance and financial journalism too? The PR spinners had convinced them that is was money for nothing and the boom was never ending. History was bunk; this would be boom with no bust.

They were wrong.

Did the Great 2008 Crash see the end of financial Gonzo (or Gung Ho) journalism or, as some called it: Playing Footsie with the FTSE? Has the financial press lost the trust of the public?

The experience one year on is not encouraging. A legacy of huge public debt, unemployment and bankruptcies up to historic figures not meant to be seen again plus some huge bank losses as well. Public finances will be in a pickle for years to come. The financial supplements of the newspapers are now a little more critical but still choc a bloc and still cheer-leaders for the new consumer capitalism. Their advertising, though, has shrunk exponentially as the new products disappear from the market along with the customers and their wallets. Journalism supped with the devil of Mammon. Journalism lost.

US Pulitzer Prize-winning journalist David Cay Johnston comes from a school of classic investigative journalism. He applies it to the performance of the financial press, especially in the USA, and concludes: All the barking by all the watchdogs at the big papers (where most serious journalism gets committed), wire services and

John Mair

magazines was drowned out by the enticing sounds from a global asset inflation party. He does not hold out much hope for the future either.

Poacher turned gamekeeper Peter Wilby, journalist and editor now media analyst on the *Guardian*, gives it some perspective. It has been said of sports journalists that they are fans with typewriters. The same can be said of business journalists who are mostly fans of capitalism and like all fan(atics) of football or the market, they can let emotion get in the way of logic If they make predictions about economic prospects in general or share prices in particular, they should be taken with the same cellars of salt as you would take the football writers' predictions of who will win Saturday's top-of-the-table match.

Jane Fuller, top financial analyst and formerly of the *Financial Times*, concurs that ignorance by the financial press is an answer too but not a justifiable one whilst top media blogger Kristine Lowe examines the crash coverage from that new coal face of journalism in the digital age – the blogosphere.

Academic Damian Tambini concludes in his piece for this *ES* special that financial and business journalism in the UK is under intense pressure due to the pressures of speed, PR, and the technical complexity of financial stories. But this is only part of the explanation of why journalists largely failed to inform us of the impeding doom. At least as important is the fact that many financial journalists reject the notion that they should act as a watchdog of the public interest.

Put simply, this watchdog never wanted to bark! Being a lapdog was simply easier and more in tune with their professional ethical stand. Faced with the biggest story of their professional lifetime, too much of the financial and the general press simply fluffed it, looked the other way and passed the ball. Ironically, one of the major casualties of the recession has been the media itself. Thousands of journalism jobs (including in business and finance) have been lost worldwide in a cull that has left much blood on newsroom carpets. An atmosphere of corporate doom is not one to encourage brave and revelatory reporting. The journalists may have slit their own throats by not barking earlier and louder.

By way of conclusion, Professor John Tulloch takes his unique helicopter view of the whole sorry situation and helps answer the big question: "Just why did so few report it properly?"

David Cay Johnston

How the US media watchdogs' barking was drowned out by the global asset inflation party

Pulitzer Prize-winner David Cay Johnston, in examining US coverage, argues that even among finance reporters none could have predicted the Great Crash of 2008 any more than a sports reporter could predict the final score before play begins. But the broad outlines of what was happening had been widely reported

For more than a decade, smart financial journalists warned what was going on. They warned about artificially inflating the prices of assets such as houses and stocks because these prices would one day have to fall back to reality, causing widespread damage. They warned about loose credit. They warned about weak regulations, lax law enforcement and such subtleties as trading ahead of customers to pocket profits unfairly. They warned about accounting rules that produce not a reasonable impression of a company's finances, but, instead, hid bad debts while erecting Potemkin villages of profit.

News clips, stacks of them, as well as books prove that long before the mortgage meltdown began in August 2007, there were journalists who were on to the story of how financial manipulation was artificially inflating assets, concentrating gains among a relative few and rewriting the government rulebook for their own advantage. Indeed, these were the themes of *Free lunch* and *Perfectly legal*, two bestselling books I wrote.

Floyd Norris, Gretchen Morgenson, Allan Sloan, Bethany McLean and I were a few among those whose bylined clips prove that we saw broadly what was happening and told. But, as we shall see, even though a few diligent financial journalists understood broadly what was going on – and wrote page one stories, magazine covers and best-selling books – their message was lost.

New breed of maths wizards
All the barking by all the watchdogs at the big papers (where most serious journalism gets committed), wire services and magazines was drowned out by the enticing sounds from a global asset

David Cay Johnston

inflation party. This party was a celebration designed by accountants, lawyers and a new breed of maths wizards known as the "financial engineers", a band pumping out high-volume tunes about riches beyond imagining with no risk, all set to a mind-numbing beat.

Guess who got listened to most in a contest between watchdog barking and the sweet music of double-digit annual returns on investments? When it comes to music, actual songs, whom do you spend more time with – the rock stars or the music critics? And if you think you give the critics much attention then put this article down, name some critics from memory and then recite a few lines from their works. But before getting too deep into why the watchdogs' barks went unheeded, let's look at the record of financial journalism in the past dozen years or so, at least in America.

Way back in 1994 the estimable Carol J. Loomis, of *Fortune* magazine, sounded a warning that derivatives could provoke a future economic crisis. In 1997, the *Oregonian* in Portland, Oregon, wrote about house prices rising faster than the incomes needed to support new mortgages. It was one of hundreds of such articles in newspapers across the country before the turn of the last century.

Growing problem of predatory lending
In March 2000 a series ran in *The New York Times* and on the ABC Television network about the growing problem of predatory lending. The principal reporter was Diana B. Henriques of *The Times*, who has a decades-long track record of getting it right and getting it early. Three years later, *The Times* reported on efforts to crack down on predatory lending, including how a dozen states had enacted laws to thwart predatory lending. In 2004, CNN's Terry Frieden wrote that "rampant fraud in the mortgage industry has increased so sharply that the FBI warned Friday of an 'epidemic' of financial crimes which, if not curtailed, could become 'the next Savings and Loans crisis'".

In mortgage lending, what was largely, but not entirely, missed was a story based on two words guaranteed to make an editor's eyes glaze over – assignee liability. Yet to understand the disaster caused by making loans that are not being paid back requires understanding the legal and economic concept captured in those two obtuse words.

Bankers got loans changed so that they were no longer responsible for the loans they made once they sold them to investment pools. They undid the old rules that said that if a loan went sour the banks had to take them back. In that simple two-word phrase is captured the essence of all the deals that have been given the label "toxic assets". By no longer having to take back bad loans, the bankers had managed the crucial trick of separating risk from responsibility.

And that is what the financial crisis is really all about at the most basic level – separating *risk from responsibility*.

Also reported, especially in *The New York Times*, were stories on what was being done at the regulatory agencies, the white-collar crime agencies that regulate banking, stocks and bonds, markets and taxes during the era of Reaganism, 1980-2008. In America, the staffs of these agencies were cut even as the economy boomed (or seemed to boom). New internal rules thwarted initiative by the white-collar detectives of the Securities and Exchange Commission (SEC), Internal Revenue Service and bank examiners. One telling example: the SEC adopted a rule during the George W. Bush administration requiring the commission to approve the kind of formal inquiry that in the past the staff would have undertaken on their own; but for that rule, the staff might well have acted on tips and exposed Bernie Madoff's Ponzi scheme five or so years sooner.

How Reagan's policies handcuffed the white-collar police

Think of these Reaganism policies as simultaneously handcuffing the white-collar police while reorganising them to make sure the staff assigned to the petty theft squad was bigger than the financial equivalent of the homicide squad. In America this trend became so distorted that for several years the poor were more likely than the prosperous to have their tax returns audited.

In journalism, today as always, covering how government works is a beat with limited appeal to the audience. Too few journalists have studied public administration, management theory and other issues that would enable them to see how the inner workings of government affect our lives and then also have the skill to make this inherently boring work interesting enough to get on to page one or even into print.

Even among the reporters who have such skills, none could possibly have predicted exactly what transpired, anymore than a sports reporter could predict the final score before play begins. But the broad outlines of what was happening, and many telling details, were widely reported. No special skills were needed to cover the politicians who warned that the new policies were a recipe for future disaster. "This legislation is just fundamentally terrible," Senator Bryon Dorgan, Democrat of North Dakota, warned as New Deal rules that segregated retail banks, investment banks and insurers were replaced with a new law sought by Wall Street in 1999.

But the law passed, overwhelmingly, and that changed the story. Journalists do not pass laws, politicians do. And while journalists can (and in this case did) point out facts, examples and scenarios under which the new rules could prove to be disastrous, once the lawmakers make new law then society has to live with that law, be it a boon to society or a disaster.

The better question is why, and how, did so many lawmakers get wrapped up in bad policy ideas – and why have they not corrected the structural problems that helped produce the Great Recession? None of this is to suggest that most journalists got it. They did not. There are much larger stacks of clips, as well as books, filled with reporting on the financial markets, the new laws and the rise of financial engineering that range from the gullible to the Panglossian.

How the WSJ dismissed warning of a housing bubble
David Wessel, economics editor of the *Wall Street Journal*, wrote a column in June 2002 dismissive of those who saw a housing bubble forming – and without quoting any of those raising concerns. "Rest easy, all ye homeowners: Housing prices don't yet look like a bubble of dot-com dimensions," Wessel wrote, relying heavily on the presumed wisdom of Federal Reserve chairman Alan Greenspan. Wessel dismissed concerns that housing prices were rising faster than incomes, calling that a "crude attempt" to apply the price-earnings ratio used to evaluate stocks to housing and adding: "Analysts who see a housing-price bubble cite economic fact and pop psychology."

On the new financial channels on television, it is always a time of softball questions to CEOs, eternal optimism about the upward direction of stock prices and constant preaching about faith in markets, the new gods who will magically deliver manna if we just praise them enough. Gather by the millions, investors do before the electronic shrines in our living rooms, offices, bars and trading desks and turn to the channels promoting the gospel of the House of Mammon. From the electronic pew we study anew each day the new divine scriptures in the daily flood of data from the Dow Jones Industrial Average and all the other indexes that can purify faith.

From the rare and glorified words of the Oracle of Omaha to the incessant sermons delivered by the parish priests of CNBC, Bloomberg and Fox Business News, those seeking riches without work tune in to hear the Gospel of Greed. They seek to profit by studying the patterns of the charts of daily prices and also of the moving averages of days 50 and 200. The preachers and the guests invited to deliver sermonettes rail endlessly against the oppressive hand of government. And in all they focus on the instant return, the speculative profit, the gain from trading, rather than from the building of substantial enterprises that create wealth through insight, hard work and delivering quality goods and services.

There are many temples in the House of Mammon, some of them too big to fail, like AIG, Bank of America and Citibank, the original one-stop financial supermarket. The grandest temple in the House of Mammon is Goldman Sachs, whose influence reaches into so many places that the writer Matt Taibbi said trying to chart its connections was like trying to make a chart of everything.

In the House of Mammon: Let us prey

Goldman, the beneficiary of $13 billion of bailout money it said it did not need but kept, specialises in trading and also in financing the selling and reselling of companies to gather our fees. But in every corner of the House of Mammon the call is the same: let us prey. Even if we operated from cold-blooded rationality at all times on matters financial, we live in a world drenched in competing media bidding for our attention. We are, in fact, supersaturated with messages; so many that they bounce off us like so many bubbles in soft drink.

The bottom line: all the insightful journalism in the world cannot overcome bad government policies, especially those that ignore thousands of years of history about the need to audit, regulate and inspect financial institutions. And those bad policies trace back to the rise of the political donor class, the very rich and very thin slice of citizens who finance campaigns. Their voices get heard first and foremost. Their concerns get reflected in law more than those of everyone else. And what is fair to them may be profoundly unfair to the rest of us, whether we listened to the barking watchdogs or not. And even if you had paid close attention would you have invested differently?

Our mistake is thinking that we can throw a global asset inflation party, to the drumbeat of the "financial engineers" band, free of risks and certainly free of responsibilities. Before the game begins, no one expects the sports reporter to know the final score. Yet the Great Crash brings cries of "Why didn't the financial reporters warn us our stocks and homes would collapse?"

News flash: You were warned. Again and again and again.

Note on Contributor
David Cay Johnston won a Pulitzer Prize for exposing tax loopholes and a George Polk award for exposing political spying by the Los Angeles Police Department. In 2008, he left *The New York Times* and now teaches the law of the ancient world at Syracuse University College of Law and writes columns for Tax Notes and the *Nation*.

Peter Wilby

When business journalism gets in bed with the financial institutions

Peter Wilby, media commentator on the *Guardian*, argues that it's unfair to blame financial journalists for their failure to predict the crisis. The press in general and its employees had a vested interest in the "irrational exuberance" that preceded the financial crisis

During my 40-plus years in journalism, I learned one lesson very early: never take advice from the office experts. Do not ask the property correspondent which house to buy, the motoring correspondent which car to choose, the gardening columnist which flowers to plant, or the education correspondent which school to send your child to. And above all, do not ask business and finance writers where to invest your money.

The world financial crisis exposed the failures not only of government, regulatory bodies and banking but also of journalism. Nine months before Northern Rock collapsed in September 2007, *The Times* heralded "a new era of bigger returns for shareholders" from a company "firing on all cylinders". The same paper gave the launch of Northern Rock's "silver savings online account" for the over-50s "an unequivocal thumbs up" even after the bank had issued its June profits warning. As late as August, the *Telegraph* assured readers that customers were safe and that Northern Rock offered a "compelling combination" of potential dividend yields at low cost.

Journalists performed little better over the following year as the Icelandic banks headed towards their collapse in autumn 2008. Several listed Heritable, Kaupthing and Landsbanki (Icesave) in their "best buy" savings tables until the weekend before those banks crashed. Personal finance sections failed to explain that, if a bank comes top of such tables, its high interest rates probably represent what financiers call "a risk premium", which compensates investors for the chance they will lose everything. Nor did they explain that a government money-back guarantee was of little use if the state, like Iceland, also risked bankruptcy. Some journalists had the grace to apologise for their errors, though it was hardly reassuring when they added that they or their families had themselves put money into Northern Rock or the Icelandic banks.

When it came to their annual share tips for 2008, the year when the FTSE100 would plunge by roughly one third, journalists' performance was equally lamentable. The *Telegraph* tipped Yell, British Land, Punch Taverns and Standard Chartered, all of which fell more than the FTSE generally, by amounts ranging from 39 per cent to 92 per cent. *The Sunday Times* advised putting money into the Brazilian, Israeli and Russian stock markets, which fell by 38 per cent, 51 per cent and 72 per cent respectively in 2008.

Few suggested staying out of the stock markets

Few, if any, pundits suggested 2008 might be a good year to stay out of stock markets entirely. Even as the FTSE dipped below 6,000 – it would end the year at 4,434 – *The Times'* personal finance editor wrote that "few serious economists are predicting a UK or worldwide recession...there are reasons to believe that stock prices will not end the year lower than they are today". In January 2008, Anatole Kaletsky, the notoriously Panglossian economics columnist for *The Times*, wrote that the trouble was almost over and that stock markets "will rise in 2008". Several commentators argued that the crisis would be limited to the financial sector and would not affect the wider economy.

Curiously, some critics – notably Richard Lambert, a former *Financial Times* Editor, now Director General of the CBI – complained that by "careless headlines or injudicious reporting" ("Terror stalks the stock market", that kind of thing), journalists were guilty of "self-fulfilling prophecies of a very serious nature" which the Press Complaints Commission should attempt to curb. But if journalists were guilty of hyping up the crisis, they were far more guilty of failing to warn in advance that a long boom in financial markets rested on dubious foundations. They may have deepened the crisis somewhat but, to a far greater extent, they helped to inflate the boom by encouraging readers to pile into what looked like an ever-rising stock market.

Several commentators acknowledged this. The *Observer*'s Will Hutton said in November 2008 that journalists had "lost their senses" and "suspended their judgement". *The Financial Times* performed better than most, with its correspondent Gillian Tett emerging as just about the only journalist who grasped the dangers of a new financial instrument called "derivatives". But its Editor Lionel Barber, lecturing at Yale University in April 2009, said "financial journalists were too slow to grasp that a crash in the banking system would have a profoundly damaging impact on the real economy".

Peter Wilby

Outright criminal behaviour

What accounts for this failure? This is not a trivial matter since we are talking about people's livelihoods, homes, pensions and lifetime savings. A small number of high-flying financiers, by reckless and sometimes dishonest, greedy or even outright criminal behaviour, threatened to ruin us all. We were, we are now told, within a whisker of every bank locking its doors and shutting down its cash machines, plunging us back to the age of barter. If ever there was a case for journalistic whistleblowing, this was it. And a few far-sighted journalists – such as Tett and *The Times* and *New Statesman* columnist Patrick Hosking – warned of trouble ahead. So did some reputable economists and financiers, such as Ann Pettifor, of the New Economics Foundation, who wrote in the *New Statesman* in 2003 (when I was editor) of a growing "crisis of debt and deflation".

But like the UN inspector Scott Ritter, who insisted before the Iraq war began that the Iraqi President Saddam Hussein had no weapons of mass destruction, they were largely ignored and treated as marginal, slightly eccentric figures. Journalists went with the consensus, as they often do. Dissenters were often dismissed as the agents of leftist conspirators, intent on undermining capitalism. Journalists accepted what the captains of industry, finance and politics told them: that slumps had been abolished and the bubble would never burst. The comparison with Iraq, where journalism also largely failed, is indeed a telling one. As a senior *New Yorker* editor put it, "business journalism was in bed with, or embedded, in the [financial] institutions the way that war correspondents were embedded in the units in Iraq".

Some of the failure was simply the result of ignorance. Being a banking correspondent isn't like being an education or health correspondent where you are likely to be as well paid (or at least not hugely worse paid) than most of the people you are writing about. Any journalist who fully understood the workings of financial markets would be inside the game making a small fortune, not on the outside reporting it. Indeed, many of the brighter business writers have in recent years been seduced into the financial services industry to work as PRs. But even basic skills – which might enable them to see that something is amiss without knowing exactly what it is – are frequently lacking. Few journalists, even business journalists, are very numerate and, as Barber acknowledged, most have a weak grasp of accounting practice and can't, to put it crudely, read a balance sheet.

Investigations costly, time-consuming and uncertain of outcome

Then there is the lack of resources from which all newspapers increasingly suffer. Investigations into financial affairs are time-consuming and uncertain of outcome, particularly given the readiness with which rich corporations reach for their lawyers. The result may make waves, but it rarely provides what an editor would consider a good, racy read. And so arcane are many corporate accounts that, even after the most careful and thorough checks, a newspaper may still get the wrong end of the stick, as the *Guardian* found with its investigation into Tesco's use of tax avoidance schemes.

These constraints were significant factors in the newspapers' inability to give early warning of impending disaster. But the "embedding" factor – journalists' willingness to accept the conventional wisdom in the industry they covered – was by far the most important. I do not intend to imply outright corruption by pointing out that most newspapers, particularly the upmarket ones, receive substantial revenues from, for example, property advertising or bank advertising of mortgages, savings accounts and other "financial products". Nor do I suggest that advertisers can successfully threaten to withdraw support if there is negative coverage; the walls between editorial and advertising work tolerably well in the British nationals. But advertising is bound at least to have a subliminal effect. Property sections tend to shrink when the housing market slumps. No property journalist, therefore, will go out of his or her way to talk up the prospect of a sharp fall in house .prices. Similarly, the share tipster who advises readers that it's best to leave their money in a bog-standard savings account is writing himself or herself out of a job.

As for more general business and economics reporters, they rarely see themselves in the role of watchdogs, still less as critics of the capitalist system in general. Business sections, including the *Financial Times*, are mostly written for insiders. The *Guardian* alone places its business and finance pages (Mondays to Fridays, but not Saturdays, when it gets easily its highest readership) in the main run of news before the comment pages. The others, when they are not in separate sections, tend to be buried near the obituaries. Only the *Guardian* makes persistent attempts to expose how business rips off consumers, overpays its senior executives, underpays its workers, avoids paying tax, trashes the environment and makes deals with dictators.

Business journalists mostly fans of capitalism
It has been said of sports journalists that they are fans with typewriters. The same can be said of business journalists who are mostly fans of capitalism, just as labour correspondents (now all but extinct) were fans of trade unions. If they make predictions about economic prospects in general or share prices in particular, they should be taken with the same cellars of salt as you would take the football writers' predictions of who will win Saturday's

top-of-the-table match. All specialist journalists are vulnerable to producer capture, but business and economics writers are more vulnerable than most, because the prevailing neoliberal ideology is so all-encompassing and so pleasing to those who own and edit newspapers.

Again, like all specialist journalists, they rely on the insiders for information and potential exclusive stories. It is hard in such circumstances to retain an independent mind. Deregulation, the journalists' sources told them, was a good thing. So, as Barber argued, crucial regulatory decisions – such as a US move to loosen bank debt restrictions in 2004 – went unexamined. Derivatives, hedge funds and securitised assets, the sources said, were brilliant, innovative financial "instruments" that would usher in a new age of eternal, global prosperity. No journalist observed that these are just the latest jargon for what financial markets have been about since the Middle Ages – debt and transfer of risk.

But it is surely unfair to blame financial journalists alone. The press and its employees had a vested interest in the "irrational exuberance" that preceded the financial crisis. Despite circulation declines and the growing migration of advertising to the internet, most newspapers continued to make substantial profits. Most journalists own property and money-purchase pensions, and many also hold shares (if only through tax-free savings accounts), though a quarter of the adult population owns none of these things. If they failed to question whether the party could go on for ever, it was because they, like the people they wrote about, didn't want it to stop.

Note on Contributor
Peter Wilby is a former editor of the *New Statesman* and the *Independent on Sunday*. He is now a media commentator and *New Statesman* and *Guardian* columnist.

Jane Fuller

Why journalists need to relearn the old habits of scepticism, fearless questioning and digging for information

Top financial analyst Jane Fuller believes the credit crunch has, at least, taught journalists the need to relearn old habits – and take pride again in their independence

It is always easy for journalists to say: "Don't blame us, guv." They are observers, not actors. They simply report what is going on.

In the case of the financial crisis, which started in 2007 and is still playing out, journalists can legitimately claim that they are not the main suspects. They were not the bankers who earned enormous bonuses for selling toxic products; they were not the central bankers who failed to "take away the punchbowl" of cheap credit in a debt-fuelled boom; they were not the politicians who lied about abolishing boom and bust; and they were not the bank regulators who allowed rapid expansion with inadequate reserves.

Some have blamed journalists, notably Robert Peston, Business Editor of the BBC, for spreading panic. This, too, is easy to rebut. Being first to report something important – the emergency support that Northern Rock needed – is what every journalist strives to do. With a few exceptions under the heading of national security, it is in the public interest that they succeed. Journalists were not to blame for Northern Rock's lack of access to funds and inadequate protection of depositors.

But this defence is not good enough. It is like pretending that history can be objective when the simple act of selecting facts marks the beginning of a limited – and so potentially misleading or biased – view of events. Journalism is about more than reporting. Indeed, in the era of "real-time" information, the only way to justify anything other than instant web or broadcast news is to add analysis and comment.

Jane Fuller

Some did see it coming
Once journalists enter the arena of expert punditry, they expose themselves to the question: why didn't you see it coming? The answer is that some did. At the *Financial Times*, the following trends were reported on at length:

- the rise in house prices to historically high levels when compared with such factors as borrowers' income;
- the growing trade imbalance between importing nations, such as the US and UK, and exporters such as China, and the related stretched funding of consumer nations' debts;
- easy credit and the mispricing of risk: from credit card holders to private equity firms, debt was too easy to obtain and interest costs low;
- the government's fiddling with the "golden rule" about only borrowing to invest and with definitions of the economic cycle.

Nevertheless, those who said it was too good to last and would all end in tears were inevitably wrong until they were proved right. The same thing happened in the dotcom stock-market bubble in the late 1990s. The most prominent doomsayer among UK fund managers, Tony Dye, quit his job in March 2000 just before it burst. John Kay, an economist and *FT* columnist, had the following answer to the question posed by the Queen about the failure to predict the crisis:

> I believed that I would win kudos for my contrarian view when the bubble burst. But people who had not wished to be told they were talking nonsense before the bubble burst did not wish to be told they had been talking nonsense after the bubble burst either. Indeed, they did not recall that they had been talking nonsense (*FT*, 30 December 2008).

The deaf ear turned to contrarians when things are going well is related to the financial markets' version of the "greater fool" theory. Everyone believes they know when asset prices are high but they also know that prices over-shoot on both the way up and the way down. They are afraid of selling too soon and missing out on boom-time profits, and they believe they are smart enough to reach the exit first when the cycle turns. They reckon they will be able to sell to a "greater fool".

"Early is the new wrong" became the catchphrase
A similar timing issue emerged in 2008 when certain investors, including sovereign wealth funds, bought stakes in US and Swiss banks. But bank share prices continued to fall as the crisis worsened. "Early is the new wrong" became a new catch-phrase

as other investors sat on the sidelines until March 2009 when prices looked unequivocally cheap. But none of this provides an excuse for journalists to avoid questioning conventional wisdom. Indeed, journalists are best placed to be contrarians because they have no financial skin in the game, are trained to inquire and should have independent minds. It is a valuable professional trait to be sceptical.

So why did many journalists unthinkingly go along with the market euphoria and complacency about the economy? Part of the answer is that they are home owners and consumers too, and so did have a financial interest in the boom. The increasing dependence on advertising revenue, as the internet undermined the ability to charge for editorial content, also gave the profession more of an interest in consumer-led economic growth.

A failure of detachment is understandable, although it should be recognised and fought, but some journalistic failures were dumb. It is not the job of journalists to do a marketing job, whether the goods for sale be a house, a company's shares or a piece of clothing. The line between editorial and advertorial, or "puff pieces", needs to be redrawn, and when journalists pass comment on anything that is for sale, it should be clear that it is just that: only an opinion. Another aspect of dumb journalism is hero worship. It is the role of a famous person's publicist to omit or gloss over the great one's faults. A journalist should always ask the difficult, and even rude, questions.

In terms of culpability, sins of omission are more insidious than the rather obvious cheer-leading that some journalists got sucked into. Ignoring the elephant in the room is a cliché that should never lose its meaning for the profession. A related one, which ties the trunk to the legs and the tail, is that journalists must do "joined-up thinking".

Complicitous silence – the most dangerous trap for journalists

Gillian Tett, an assistant editor at the *FT* and author of *Fool's gold*, uses her training as an anthropologist to explain the malfunctioning of financial markets. In a column on 21 August 2009, she quoted Pierre Bourdieu, a French sociologist, as saying: "The most successful ideological effects are those which have no need of words, and ask no more than a complicitous silence." Complicitous silence captures the most dangerous trap that journalists fall into, although it credits them with too much guile to imply that the complicity is deliberate. The reasons for journalistic omission tend to be innocent or mundane: humility, lack of time and laziness.

Jane Fuller

Take humility. Who are journalists to question Alan Greenspan, chairman of the US Federal Reserve and the man credited with clearing up the mess after previous (mini) crises? Journalists underestimate the value of their independence from the institution, process and school of thought that their expert interviewee represents. They are also too afraid of asking dumb questions (there is no such thing – although this does not excuse journalists from doing their homework). Lack of time and laziness have the same outcome: corners are cut. In the build-up to the credit crisis – and in the ongoing coverage of it – here are some of the ways this shows through:

- Dumbing down. If there is only room/time to make one point, keep it simple. For example, charges for unauthorised overdrafts are high, therefore they are not fair and should be banned. The elephant in the room is: easy credit got us into this mess, how do you deter people from borrowing more than they ought to?

- Lack of perspective – a gee-whizz point with no context. For example, Northern Rock is allowing people to borrow 125 per cent of the value of their house. Anyone remember the negative equity of the late 1980s, early 90s?

- Failure to do the sums. Too many journalist are uncomfortable with numbers. This makes them prone to be impressed by big ones, especially sales. They should remember that: sales are vanity, profit is sanity and cash is reality. Particularly dangerous in reporting on banks is balance sheet (assets/liabilities/capital) ignorance.

- Lack of joined-up thinking. Economists say that UK consumers are over-indebted and too dependent on rising house values. Reporters fail to dig down into what that means for a family being lent five or six times their income.

- Failure to ask what if? A capital markets report says that private equity firms are starting to pay eight times the profits of the companies they acquire. Those reporting individual deals fail to ask: what if profits go down and interest costs go up?

- Failure to spot behavioural changes: the sub-prime mortgage crisis started as a scandal of over-charging borrowers, often from ethnic minorities, who turned out to be good re-payers. The scandal morphed into one that involved, at best, mis-selling of mortgages to vulnerable people and at worst "liars' loans", or fraud.

This crisis will run and run...
Journalists are as well qualified as anyone to spot behavioural change and to question incentives: for instance, the higher

commissions earned by mortgage brokers who sought out sub-prime customers. Fortunately for journalists (no apology for the profession's vulture tendencies), this crisis will run and run, despite the late-summer wishful thinking that it had all blown over. So plenty of scope remains to report on the impact of: falling house prices and rising unemployment; the great wave of banking re-regulation; the inconsistency of politicians who want banks to both lend more and conserve their capital; the reduction in competition through "rescue" takeovers; bankers' bonuses…

In short, journalists need to relearn the old habits of scepticism, fearless questioning, digging for information, spotting connections and taking pride in their independence.

Note on Contributor
Jane Fuller is co-director of the Centre for the Study of Financial Innovation, a London-based think-tank. She is a former Financial Editor of the *Financial Times* and continues to train *FT* journalists. She chairs the Accounting Advocacy Committee of the CFA Society of the UK, the analysts' organisation. In 2005 she formed her own consultancy, Fuller Analysis, and her clients include the Accounting Standards Board and the *Financial Times*. She is also co-editor of *Harriman's financial dictionary*.

Kristine Lowe

How blogs challenged and transformed mainstream media coverage of the credit crisis

Financial blogs show us the extent to which the media's institutional constraints were both an asset and a major liability when covering the biggest financial story of our time, according to top media blogger Kristine Lowe

"Financial blogs have covered the events leading up to the credit crisis much better than mainstream media. And thanks to them, I have made good money from," said Björn A Jörgensen, a small-time private investor, deeply interested in macro economy.[1]

In Jörgensen's opinion, financial blogs such as Calculated Risk, Seeking Alpha, Zero Hedge and the Market Ticker have provided a more thorough, better analysis of the events, as well as covering issues earlier, often drawing parallels to historical events and looking at cause and effect relationships. As a recent example, he cites blogger Chris Martenson uncovering how the US Federal Reserve is buying huge chunks of US Treasury debt, presumably to boost the stock market.[2]

Financial blogs and journalism, a comparative analysis
"Mainstream media reporting of finance and business is still important in that it keeps everyone updated with data releases and breaking news. But its relevance and timeliness more or less stop there, and bloggers step in to fill in on the rest," said Dana Chen, a financial blogger and former analyst who is currently involved in a finance news launch.[3] Indeed, more and more people find that, in their chosen fields, specialist blogs cover issues more in-depth than traditional media. It has certainly been my experience as a media journalist that blogs such as Professor Piet Bakker's Newspaper Innovation and venture capitalist Fred Wilson's A VC cover their chosen subjects better and more consistently than their mainstream media (MSM) counterparts.

Comparing financial blogs with MSM also highlights how the latter's institutional constraints both hamper and benefit financial journalism. In his London School of Economics report, *What is financial journalism for? Ethics and responsibilities in a time of change,"*[4] Dr Damian Tambini offers a good synopsis of where these constraints can be most detrimental. He identifies four key problems facing financial journalists today, all of which may have affected the coverage of the credit crisis in a negative way. These are: 1) the speed of financial news; 2) the complexity of issues; 3) the increased power of PR strategy and 4) the limited resources of time and skill.

Examples of constraints that may be beneficial are the mainstream media's relatively clear codes of conduct and demands for verification. From an ethical perspective, blogs operate in an environment which in many respects resembles that of financial journalism in the eighties, when the City and its watchdogs were altogether less encumbered by what former Geert Linnebank, editor-in-chief of Reuters, dubbed "regulatory creep".

As we have seen from the popular political bloggers such as Guido Fawkes (aka Paul Staines),[5] bloggers sometimes go where most mainstream journalists cannot or dare not go. In the realm of financial blogging, this may imply peddling rumours irresponsibly and testing the limits for what constitutes market abuse, libel and ramping.

No legal framework
It is worth noting that there have been several initiatives to make the blogosphere adhere more to regulatory practices akin to those of MSM. Notable examples are efforts by Estonian MEP Marianne Mikko in the EU Parliament[6] and Judge Eady's recent ruling about anonymity in the Night Jack case,[7] but no legislation particularly concerning blogs currently exists.

"You would not think bloggers could move markets: we have certain rules that apply to everyone on things like market abuse and unlicensed trading in shares, but none for bloggers in particular," an FSA spokeswoman explained.[8]

A blogger's ability to move markets may, of course, depend on who the blogger is. If the person in question also happens to be the BBC's business editor it may be a very different story, as the controversy surrounding the credit crisis's star reporter Robert Peston revealed.

"Within minutes of his report of a meeting between bank chiefs and the Chancellor on Tuesday, billions of pounds were wiped off the value of Barclays, RBS and Lloyds TSB," the *Independent* wrote[9] of Peston, who later was called before the Treasury Select Committee to answer questions about his scoops on the bank collapse.[10]

"Peston is a market threat because he is considered to have so good sources in Nos 10 and 11 that his reports can send share prices to heaven or hell," asserted blogger Guido Fawkes, a former hedge fund manager, and called for Peston to be gagged.[11]

Financial journalists should not be head of queue
Stephen Kahn, the former City editor of the *Daily Express* who took early retirement in February after 30 years in the industry, had this to say on the matter: "Peston was not responsible for the Northern Rock mess. Has he been used? I do not know, I am not sure he knows either." However, given their resources, Kahn thought financial journalists did a reasonably good job. "There used to be dedicated investigative journalism teams, such as *The Sunday Times*'s Insight Team: not anymore. Peston does all this next to his regular job.

"Should we have seen the warning signs earlier? Yes, we should have. But people who count their salaries in the millions failed to do so. The Treasury, the Government, the Financial Services Authority failed to do so, they are all culpable. I am not sure why we should focus on financial journalists. Again it is a question of resources. When the whole city gang failed to see it coming, journalists should not be head of the queue," he said.[12] His sentiment rhymes with concerns raised in Tambini's survey about the effect of newsrooms' cost cuts and limited resources.

Talking up investments
In the blogosphere, credibility and authority is something you build through acting consistently in a credible manner and demonstrating your expertise in your chosen field repeatedly: rather like in Aristotelian ethics where a person becomes virtuous by consistently acting virtuously.[13]

That is not to say that all bloggers are, or strive to be, what Aristotle would describe as virtuous, only that they gain credibility through consistent behaviour. Take Guido Fawkes for instance: a free marketer, he derives much of his credibility from his willingness to dish up the dirt on politicians of all stripes, not only Labour.

In the realm of financial blogging, influential blogger Karl Denninger, who writes the Market Ticker,[14] offers an interesting example. He will often disclose that he has a short position in a company he writes a negative blog post on, and, as a result, may benefit financially if the market acts on his analysis. However, Denninger also issues the following warning to his readers: "The author may have a position in any company or security mentioned herein. Actions you undertake as a consequence of any analysis, opinion or advertisement on this site are your sole responsibility."

Undefined ethical territory

To journalists, that may seem like very dubious practice, and media organisations tend to have explicit rules prohibiting their journalists writing about shares they own. But whereas journalists are bound by a voluntary code of conduct, which Tambini found to be interpreted in different ways from newsroom to newsroom,[15] bloggers operate by an unwritten code of conduct which dictates, among other things, that you disclose your interests and ties as far as possible.[16] The example from Denninger's blog above may serve to illustrate how his transparency can work in practice.

Tambini asserts that new operators such as blogs seek a position well outside of the restrictive ethical framework that applies to financial journalism. That is true in the sense that blogging is often defined as conversation, and a blogger as someone who is simply conversing about his or her passion, but this does not place the blogger outside of the reach of legislation as we have seen with the Night Jack ruling, and when Uzbek billionaire Alisher Usmanov forced several British MPs' personal websites and blogs offline after they repeated claims made by the former British ambassador to Uzbekistan, Craig Murray.[17]

The blinding speed of information sharing

Still, with what is commonly referred to as social media – such as blogs, micro blogging and social networking sites – everyone can be their own publishers and, unaided and unverified by traditional media, news and rumours can spread across the worldwide web like electronic wildfires. A recent example is how protesters used Twitter to communicate news about the Iran uprising in the wake of the June 2009 presidential election to the world.[18]

BBC World's global head of news, Richard Sambrook, did an informal analysis of the value of this information stream and concluded that you needed a reasonable understanding social media and an above average understanding of the political situation in Iran, to really benefit from it.[19]

From this and other examples it is safe to assume that it is not your average citizen who uses social media to keep informed about a particular issue or situation. My own experiences from writing and reading media blogs suggest they mostly attract people capable of evaluating the information, usually other media obsessives – and I would be surprised if the same was not also true for financial blogs.

Publish first, check later

But this blinding speed of information sharing has other problematic aspects. Popular technology blog Techcrunch has repeatedly demonstrated a policy which comes close to publish first, verify and fact-check afterwards. After one recent example of this the *Daily Telegraph*'s Kate Day asked if the pressure to be first is not compromising accuracy. To this, the editor of Techcrunch Europe, former journalist Mike Butcher, replied that he expected his readers to hold him to account and "fact-check" his ass.[20]

Bloggers vs. journalists: a different *modus operandi*

Despite the success of commercial blogs such as technology blog Techcrunch or financial blogs such as Seeking Alpha, Zero Hedge and Breaking Views, which are subject to some of the same pressures as MSM, the vast majority of bloggers are private persons who start blogging for personal reasons. That means there are no time limits, no word limits and rarely any close ties to sources or public relations operators to pay heed to. This may also be a key to why specialist blogs often offer more thorough, in-depth coverage of issues.

Arianna Huffington, the successful founder of Huffington Post, famously said: "Bloggers suffer from Obsessive Compulsive Disorder, journalists from Attention Deficit Disorder."[21] As a journalist and blogger I find much truth in that, and find myself switching between a very different *modus operandi* when I work in a newsroom and when I blog.

This may also offer an explanation as to why financial journalists did not spot the storm brewing. "News reporting has always been vulnerable to what Peter Jay [former Economics Editor at the BBC] and John Birt [former BBC Director General] famously described as 'the bias against understanding', precisely because it tends to focus on events instead of trends," said Nick Davies, the respected author and investigative journalist when I interviewed him for my thesis many years ago.[22]

Conclusion

Given the media's "bias against understanding" we should perhaps not be surprised that MSM largely failed to predict the great crash of 2008. Still, Thomas Friedman, the author and *New York Times* columnist, argues that in this world of increasing complexity, if you do not see the connections you do not see the world.[23] That means either financial journalists need to become experts, or MSM needs to bring more experts on board. Dana Chen argues that the latter is already happening:

> Nowadays, most serious mainstream finance-leaning media outlets have professional bloggers on staff (Megan McCardle, Ezra Klein, Felix Salmon). They tend to report, and more importantly, follow up on issues they are interested in or specialise in. That way, instead of choppy reporting here and there by this or that reporter, readers can follow "points of views" over the course of weeks and months. There's no

back-pedalling or vagueness, readers will, and do hold those bloggers accountable for their views and ideas.

Notes

1 Interview via telephone 13 August 2009.

2 http://www.chrismartenson.com/martensonreport/five-horsemen http://www.chrismartenson.com/martensoninsider/martenson-insider-fed-pomo-activity-and-stock-market.

3 Interview via email 18 August 2009. Dana Chen blogs at http://www.investoralist.com/ and is site and community manager for Viewsflow, an upcoming business and financial commentary service.

4 Tambini, Damian (2008) *What is financial journalism for?* London, Polis.

5 http://www.guardian.co.uk/media/2007/jul/09/mediatop1002007.mondaymediasection78?gusrc=rss&feed=media .

6 http://www.europarl.europa.eu/sides/getDoc.do?language=EN&type=IM-PRESS&reference=20080605STO30955.

7 Judge Eady refused to grant in June 2009 an order to protect the anonymity of the police officer who is the author of the award-winning NightJack blog. See http://technology.timesonline.co.uk/tol/news/tech_and_web/the_web/article6509677.ece.

8 Information request to the FSA's press office via telephone Friday, 14 August.

9 http://www.independent.co.uk/news/media/tv-radio/peston-finds-his-voice-and-now-the-citys-ears-are-burning-958351.html.

10 The Treasury Select Committee ran an inquiry into the banking crisis in early 2009, inviting comments on "the role of the media in financial stability and whether financial journalists should operate under any form of reporting restrictions during banking crises".

11 http://order-order.com/2008/10/07/pesto-wire-causes-more-misery/.

12 Interview 3 March 2009 via telephone.

13 Aristotle: *Nicomachean Ethics*, Penguin Classics. See also: http://en.wikipedia.org/wiki/Nicomachean_Ethics.

14 http://market-ticker.denninger.net/.

15 Tambini, Damian (op cit).

16 http://www.cyberjournalist.net/news/000215.php.

17 http://www.boingboing.net/2007/09/22/uzbek-billionarie-us.html.

18 http://www.readwriteweb.com/archives/dear_cnn_please_check_twitter_for_news_about_iran.php.

19 http://sambrook.typepad.com/sacredfacts/2009/06/twittering-the-uprising.html.

20 Exchange from a panel debate at Media140, 20 May 2009, on Twitter and journalism, which I covered for the Norwegian Online News Association (NONA). See http://netthoder.wordpress.com/2009/05/24/netthode-pa-twitter-konferanse-i-london/.

21 http://sambrook.typepad.com/sacredfacts/2007/12/quotes-of-the-y.html.

22 Interviewed via mail September 2001, for my Masters thesis Drugs and the media: A neat black and white picture? City University, London, 2001.

23 Friedman, Thomas (2000) *The Lexus and the olive tree*, New York, Anchor Books

Kristine Lowe

Note on Contributor
Kristine Lowe is a media business reporter and blogger who writes for a number of British, American and Norwegian publications and news sites, mainly on media finance and editorial development. She is also the founder and leader of the Norwegian Online News Association (NONA), a network for online media professionals.

John Tulloch

From amnesia to apocalypse: Reflections on journalism and the credit crunch

> It is this deep blankness is the real thing strange.
> The more things happen to you the more you can't
> Tell or remember even what they were.
> The contradictions cover such a range...
> (William Empson 1949)

> ...there are no tests that reliably distinguish between genuine and feigned amnesia
> (Daniel Schacter 2001: 87)

The progress of capitalism depends on amnesia – the capacity to forget the last crash/slump/bust so that we can help the old creep slide into one more exuberant turn on the dance floor. Any trust we repose in the financial system depends on this process of forgetting, and a suspension of that anxiety which most of us experience when we force ourselves to confront matters financial. Although the present crisis appears to be, we are told, the most severe economic downturn since 1945, the UK has suffered eight recessions since that date – defined as a fall in output for two consecutive quarters (Buckley 2009; Ferguson 2008).[1] The UK is not alone. The Harvard economist Robert Barro, as reported by Niall Ferguson, "has identified 148 crises since 1870 in which a country experienced a cumulative decline in gross domestic product (GDP) of at least 10 per cent, implying a probability of financial disaster of around 3.6 per cent per year" (Ferguson 2009c, 343). Indeed, we might agree with Hyman Minsky up to a point that "the essential critical flaw in capitalism is instability" (Minsky 1982: 86) or, as Ferguson puts it – with a bold assertion of self-interest:

> For reasons to do with human psychology and the failure of most educational institutions to teach financial history, we are always more amazed when such things happen than we should be (Ferguson 2009a).

But courses in financial history, though worthwhile and revealing, are unlikely to check the speculative manias that have characterised capitalism. And we might note that the instability identified by

John Tulloch

Minsky masks the inability of the system to eliminate poverty and the anxieties that afflict large sections of the community about their economic prospects. Let's be candid with the truism: the essential critical flaw in capitalism is that it keeps many people obscenely poor, and some insanely rich.

In our routine social interactions we attribute amnesia to a host of factors: old age, general stupidity, selective perception, self deception, physical disorders of the brain, mental illness, other problems with perception and, with Ferguson, an ignorance of history. In addition we know from our own experience that amnesia can be routinely feigned – as was for example suspected of Rudolf Hess at the Nuremberg trials, where Hess appeared not to recognise Herman Goering (Bigger 2006: 50-52). We also know that forgetting can be rashly deliberate – a refusal to face reality – as the Nobel prizewinning economist Paul Krugman observes of the crunch: "At a fundamental level…we're paying the price for wilful amnesia. We chose to forget what happened in the 1930s –and having refused to learn from history, we're repeating it" (Krugman 2008).

The Harvard psychologist and authority on memory, Daniel Schacter, more precisely describes these traits of forgetting as "the seven sins of memory" and terms them: transience, absent mindedness, blocking, misattribution, persistence, suggestibility, bias and persistence. (Schacter 2001: 4) In various ways, all these traits have operated in the current crisis.

From irrational exuberance to irrational pessimism
But amnesia is out of fashion, temporarily. We have crashed from irrational exuberance into irrational pessimism (Blastland and Dilnot 2008). And a crash course in financial history is something that successful transatlantic media dons such as Ferguson, Nobel economics laureates like Paul Krugman and mainstream economic commentators such as Larry Elliott have been providing since the credit crunch (Ferguson 2008, 2009a, 2009b; Krugman 2008; Elliott 2009). How vain Gordon Brown's claim to have abolished boom and bust! How easily demolishable his later claim to have meant "Tory boom and bust" (Pearson 2008; Channel 4 2008). The press and the blogosphere is full of articles recalling everything from Tulipmania, the crash of Overend and Gurney in 1866 to 1929 and the enduring perspicacity of J. K. Galbraith.

Charles Mackay's durable classic, *Extraordinary popular delusions and the madness of crowds* (1852) becomes fashionable again, with its portraits of the heyday of the South Sea and other bubbles and "the overbearing insolence of ignorant men, who had risen to sudden wealth by successful gambling, [making] men of true gentility of mind and manners blush that gold should have power to raise the unworthy in the scale of society" (Mackay 1995/1852: 71). Recently, the Reuters website ran a slideshow titled "The ghosts of 1929" using classic images by Walker Evans and others (Reuters 2008; MacMillan 2008). The *Guardian's* Chris McGreal has been (August 2009) exploring John Steinbeck's fictional journey down Route 66 in *The grapes of wrath* (McGreal 2009). We're on a nostalgia trip, to Great Crashes we had tried to forget!

As the historians tell us, despite the shrill warnings of apocalypse, there is nothing extraordinary or singular about the asset inflation, credit crunch and the failure of the banking system and state regulation that it illuminates. One doesn't have to go bodysnatching in Highgate cemetery to recall that crisis is endemic in a market capitalist system. Although the symptoms re-present themselves in protean form, the modern consequences tend to be the same – avalanche journalism which identifies guilty actors, mass unemployment and an increase in poverty and social inequality. Fred Goodwin and assorted bonus-hungry bankers and shady city operators have served as handy scapegoats for the …er… bankruptcy of the system.

All that is solid has not melted into air

Although the system may be bankrupt and propped up by the state it's still rudely there. All that is solid has not melted into air. And many voices urge us that we've been here before. British culture, in particular, has some ready models to hand. For example: a fortuitous BBC adaptation in 2008 sparked yet another rediscovery of Little Dorrit. "Part-murder mystery, part-love story, and wholly entertaining, Little Dorrit promises to be an autumn treat," gushed the BBC's head of series and serials, boosting Andrew Davies' adaptation (BBC 2008), and ignoring the wonderfully serviceable figure of Mr Merdle, the taciturn banker at the heart of that novel (BBC 2009).

> …Mr Merdle came home, from his daily occupation of causing the British name to be more and more respected in all parts of the civilised globe, capable of the appreciation of world-wide commercial enterprise and gigantic combinations of skill and capital. For, though nobody knew with the least precision what Mr Merdle's business was, except that it was to coin money, these were the terms in which everybody defined it on all ceremonious occasions, and which it was the last new polite reading of the parable of the camel and the needle's eye to accept without inquiry (Dickens 1857, Book 1, Ch 33).

Merdle is, of course, a crook and con-man and a triumphant satiric creation fiercely pursued by Dickens up to his end in a blood-spattered bath as "simply the greatest Forger and the greatest Thief that ever cheated the gallows". Absent-mindedly, throughout the book, he seems to try on imaginary handcuffs. But he is less reminiscent of the theatrical roguery of Cap'n Bob Maxwell than the New York financier Bernie Madoff – great cunning is combined with a profound blankness. [Merdle] "arises in the novel as the incarnation of the universal fantasy of having enough money to exorcise the neurotic spectre of debt…he is money incarnate" (Herbert 2002: 202). Like money, he always gives the impression of wanting to be somewhere else. This great novel explores the nature of the profoundest taboo in Victorian society – not sex but the ambivalences around money getting. To the anxiety-ridden Victorian middle classes, financial ruin seemed a daily possibility via a crooked bank or an unwise investment.

Dickens has plenty of fun with guilt and based his Merdle on the real-life financier John Sadleir MP, creator of the Tipperary bank (Schlicke 1999: 380; Ackroyd 1990: 757; Douglas-Fairhurst 2008) but the extraordinary resonance of the novel lies in his refusal to relax into a conventional account of individual villainy and his creation of a vision of an interlocking system in which Merdle is simply a representative – an unreflective and miserable puppet – of a general disease: speculative greed compounded by the snobbery of money worship. Merdle is on everybody's tongue, we are told, but, as many critics have observed, he is literally a man built out of shit (Herbert op.cit). It's worth recalling that Dickens's alternative title for the novel was *Nobody's fault*: which both captures the hypocrisy of a financial and governmental system whose reflex is to move blame around like money and the deeper truth that everyone is implicated in the system to some degree.

The role of journalism
Just what should be the role of journalism in the run-up to a crash? Some might say: to avoid the blame of having initiated it. But surely, in an ideal world, the role of journalism in all this would be to warn about impending catastrophe, identify the guilty, analyse the systemic causes, recuperate the memory of past depressions, and promote practical solutions to the endemic instability of the system and its poverty-creating potential. Conceivably a fully alert, predictive journalism might expose the dangers of an inflating asset bubble and nurse a slow deflation rather than explosive decompression.

Dream on. The crunch and the crash have produced some remarkable journalism but also a potent sense of journalism's failure. Apart from the rediscovery of the impact of the 1929-32 crash (evident, for example, in Chris McGreal's remarkable American pieces), there has been a mainstreaming of economic history and efforts to contextualise the global crisis. Most notable here has been the indefatigable Niall Ferguson, with articles spanning the Atlantic in leading US and UK publications including the *New Yorker*, *Vanity*

Fair, the *Daily Telegraph*, mainly derived from his bestselling book *The ascent of money*. However, much of the post-crash journalism has adopted a "find the guilty men" approach. As Claire Oldfield observes in an Editorial Intelligence Report, "it was a good way for non-financial journalists to wade into the recession without having to understand much about the property crash, the odd financial instruments connected to it, and the banks with dodgy mortgage debt.' (Oldfield 2009) but the approach is notable in the work of many specialists as well, such as Alex Brummer in the *Daily Mail*.

Brummer's latest book similarly takes no prisoners, titled *The crunch: How greed and incompetence sparked the credit crisis* (Brummer 2009). This is tough, persuasive journalism – pretty uncomfortable for the *Daily Mail* – but the ceaseless harping on villains lets the system off the hook. If they *hadn't* been grotesquely overpaid and incompetent, would we have avoided a credit crisis? Given the historical evidence, this is implausible. As Anthony Hilton in the *Evening Standard* observed: "Outrageous though the Goodwin pension is, there are more important things to worry about: people should stop behaving like passengers on the Titanic in a fury because the captain of the vessel has been spotted taking a free drink" (*Evening Standard,* 2 March 2009 – quoted in Oldfield 2009). Other commentators have avoided being pulled into the "guilty men" approach. For example, the *Guardian*'s Larry Elliott, has consistently avoided personalisation in favour of a systemic interpretation (Elliott 2009).

Most reflection on the role of journalism after the event has been broadly supportive of "the commentariat" – for example, Editorial Intelligence's report on *The credit crunch commentariat* (Oldfield 2009). Although *mea culpas* (or *meae culpae*) by journalists have not exactly abounded, there have been some striking efforts to identify the weaknesses in journalism revealed by the crash, notably by Danny Schechter (2009), who highlights what he terms the "embedding" of financial journalists. But what are the issues?

The five principal issues
The idea that journalism could do much to reform or mitigate the speculative manias of global capitalism is, of course, nearly as laughable as the notion that regulations hatched in the aftermath of a bubble would serve that purpose. But there are peculiar difficulties in tasking financial journalism with a reforming role. These boil down to five principal issues:

1. The origin of modern Western journalism lies in serving the needs of capitalist markets for price sensitive information relating to investment decisions with reasonable predictive power. Financial journalism is embedded in, and financially

dependent on, a system which is chronically unstable and favours "good news" stories. It is therefore an error to assume that financial journalism can have a rational function in predicting economic crises, and placing market events in historical context since, with few exceptions, financial journalism is an accomplice to the market. Predictive capacity requires a critical stance vis-à-vis the market.

2. Financial journalism is not predicated on helping to oversee or regulate the market, but to serve it. Specialist areas have an interest in asset inflation – in particular, by cheerleading increases in property and stock prices. Although there were notable and distinguished exceptions, Schechter is broadly right to argue that journalists in the prelude to the current crisis were accomplices in creating an "environment of greed and free market bullishness" and that "the newspaper industry became, in some communities, the marketing arm of the real-estate industry" (Schechter op cit, 21), the prime agency of bubbledom. But it has ever been so, and Schechter is wrong to imply that there was ever a golden age of critical financial journalism.

3. Financial journalism acts as a megaphone to magnify booms and busts, oscillating between irrational exuberance and irrational pessimism. Will Hutton argues that "Journalists for the most part missed the build-up to the crisis and did not warn the public. We all kind of believed that we had fallen upon some kind of alchemy, that capitalism had changed, and I think everyone got carried away" (quoted by Schechter op cit 24). That sounds pretty lame from a commentator as distinguished as Hutton. However, because of the net, the potential dangers of a poor or "rogue" prediction to journalists' reputations is enhanced – this breeds caution, as does the fact that critical comment will be in the nature of things, price sensitive, and Merdles come armoured in praetorian guards of lawyers.

4. In the up phase of a boom, financial journalism boosts significant individual actors. The newly minted Merdles *de nos jours* are lauded and endowed with charisma. The market system requires a continuing flow of new investors who are relatively ignorant and will buy into charisma. One function of financial journalism is to shepherd new entrants into the market via Celebrity Avenue.

5. In the down phase, financial journalism (and the rest of the news media) demonises individual actors and focuses on particular crooks rather than the crookedness of the system. While specialist financial journalism provides effective

exposés of individual bad buys (The You and Yours syndrome) it precludes an overall critical stance. In failing to address systemic issues, it focuses on the wrong problems – e.g. on house price inflation rather than a lack of housing and a lack of construction and issues in the tax system that stop people from moving.

The most sustained and self-critical reflection so far has come from Lionel Barber, who explored in a Poynter Fellowship lecture at Yale the question of how much the crisis represented a failure of journalism (Barber 2009). On the whole, Barber struggles to exonerate journalism from charges of being asleep on the job or complicit in the crisis. He argues that journalists were not alone in missing the vital signs and that the initial crisis in the banking system was "a highly technical story" originating in the credit markets – "a backwater" with little day-to-day news interest. This slides over the issue that 1. it *was* their job and 2. as with all financial journalism, the struggle to make the technical interesting goes with the territory. But he concedes that financial journalists were more interested in "good" news stories and had little interest in pursuing scandals.

When journalists "suspended their critical faculties"

Rather than systemic failures however, Barber is keen to focus on very detailed weaknesses in financial journalism. These include a failure to grasp the danger of not regulating derivatives and a lack of scrutiny of state backed homeloan operations (the evocatively named Fanny Mae and Freddy Mac and by extension the UK building societies) because wider home ownership had become a sacred cow. He also concedes that journalists did not appreciate the significance of loosened regulations re leverage for banks and that a banking crash "would have a profoundly damaging impact on the real economy" – i.e. they treated the financial sector and the real economy as "parallel universes" which would not impact on each other. Most damagingly, he concedes that journalists "suspend[ed]...critical faculties" and "followed the natural tendency to seek rationales for events as they unfold, rather than question whether they are sustainable". This is opaque speech which we might translate as: journalists failed to ask fundamental critical questions while in the midst of reassuring asset inflation. Who wants to call fire at the swingiest party since the 1920s?

Barber's solutions come down to more training, hiring journalists with better knowledge of specialist fields but at the same time eliminating what he terms the "silos" between different specialisms. Also, journalists must be aware of the "dangers in linear thinking" – another opaque reference, which presumably refers to the need for a proper apprehension of a market economy's tendency towards chaos.

John Tulloch

The moral of this, I guess, is when in doubt – in fact, when in deep deep trouble – loudly call for more training. Plainly, financial journalism is in a difficult place. And plainly, as Barber suggests, journalists should learn to read balance sheets and some accountancy techniques. "But there are no reports of journalists rushing to enrol of accountancy courses," as Peter Wilby (2009), media commentator on the *Guardian*, noted. Liberal freemarket capitalism looks a bad investment at the moment. But its problems relate to the whole practice of journalism and a crisis of public service and reliable public information. Out of all the analytical pieces on our present problems, I find the most powerfully resonant and suggestive is Ian Jack's meditation in a recent weekly column "Money is the strongest taboo in Britain" which commences with the deceptive understatement: "Some of us have gone through life not knowing enough about money" (Jack 2008) an uncanny echo of the opening sentence of Kafka's *Trial* in the venerable translation by the Muirs: "Someone must have been telling lies about Joseph K., for without having done anything wrong he was arrested one fine morning" (Kafka 1974).

Jack links the "taboo" on talking about one's own Money – which he reckons is just as forbidden for us as it was for Dickens' Victorians and worse than talking about Death (which of course has replaced the Victorian taboo on talking about Sex) – with our appalling lack of understanding of the financial world.

The gods of revolution are not summoned...

This all seems very British – and sane – in the timidity of its expectations and the realism with which it confronts fundamental anxieties that most of us share. The gods of revolution are not summoned. We know the financial system will not be decisively reformed – we're too terrified by the consequences of killing it off. But 2009 may at least go down as the year in which this British taboo on talking about our own and other people's money was decisively breached – the revelations about bonuses, together with the *Telegraph*'s superb exposé of MPs' expenses, have surely shunted us in the direction of greater transparency. One side of this of course is voyeurism – the crucial attraction of the revelations about bonuses, pensions and expenses is the gloating/envious/angry insight into how other people live. How dare they! But the other side is realism – the concrete lesson provided in the facts of inequality. Or as Jack much more persuasively puts it:

> A friend once said to me that the world would become a better place if everybody had to wear a badge declaring what they earned: "I'm a £65,000-a-year man" And so forth. I don't know. The envy and hatred generated might reduce the country to ashes. Here, because I'm writing a little about my

new relationship with money, it seems only fair to disclose some amounts. But the taboo is very strong. All I will say is that, bearing the average wage in mind, my earnings would excite envy in many people and pity in a few; that I have savings but no debts; and that my pension, when it comes, will be mainly supplied by the state.

A timid baring of the soul perhaps, but positively Orwellian in its feel for the nervous reality of our daily existence in a world where trust in financial and political institutions is at an all time laughable low.

Note
[1] 1956; 1957;1961;1973 and 1974;1975;1980 and 1981;1990 and 1991 – see http://www.telegraph.co.uk/finance/financetopics/recession/4320908/UK-recession-How-does-this-one-compare-to-those-since-1945.html, accessed on 15 August 2009

References
Ackroyd, Peter (1990) *Dickens*, London, Sinclair-Stevenson

Barber, Lionel (2009) *FT*'s Lionel Barber on why journalists "missed" the impending financial crisis, Poynter Fellowship Lecture at Yale University, Available online at http://www.poynter.org/forum/view_post.asp?id=13910, accessed on 11 August 2009

BBC (2008) Little Dorrit: cast announced for major BBC One Dickens adaptation http://www.bbc.co.uk/pressoffice/pressreleases/stories/2008/05_may/06/dorrit.shtml, accessed on 13 August 2009

BBC (2009) Madoff scandal "echoes Dickens", Radio 4 *Today*. Available online at http://news.bbc.co.uk/today/hi/today/newsid_7785000/7785365.stm, accessed on 13 August 2009

Bigger, Philip J. (2006) *Negotiator: The life and career of James B. Donovan*, Lehigh University Press

Blastland, Michael and Dilnot, Andrew (2008) Crash! Boom! Disaster! That's enough crazy talk . If we are not careful, everyone is going to start believing the ludicrously overheated rhetoric about the economy, *The Times*, 21 October p. 24

Brummer, Alex (2009) *The crunch: How greed and incompetence sparked the credit crisis*, London, Random House

Brummer, Alex (2009a) The fat cats are back. As governments dither over financial reforms, the bankers who caused the credit crunch are stashing away new fortunes, *New Statesman*, 6 August

Buckley, George (2009) UK recession: How does this one compare to those since 1945? *Daily Telegraph*, 23 January. Available online at http://www.telegraph.co.uk/finance/financetopics/recession/4320908/UK-recession-How-does-this-one-compare-to-those-since-1945.html, accessed on 13 August 2009

Channel 4 News (2009) FactCheck: no more boom and bust?
Available online at http://www.channel4.com/news/articles/politics/domestic_politics/factcheck+no+more+boom+and+bust/2564157, accessed on 13 August 2009

Dickens, Charles (1857) *Little Dorrit*, London, Chapman and Hall

Douglas-Fairhurst, Robert (2008) Financial crisis: We should turn to Charles Dickens in hard times, not just Little Dorrit, *Daily Telegraph*, 21 October. Available online at http://www.telegraph.co.uk/culture/books/3562382/Financial-crisis-We...d-turn-to-Charles-Dickens-in-hard-times-not-just-Little-Dorrit.html, accessed on 13 August 2009

Elliott, Larry (2009) It's a funny old game,: where is the dream team of economists to tackle the slump? *Guardian*, 1 June p. 22

Empson, William (1949/2000) "Let it go" in the *Complete Poems*, Haffenden, John (ed.) London, Allen Lane p. 99

Ferguson, Niall (2008) Wall Street lays another egg, *Vanity Fair*, December. Available online at http://www.vanityfair.com/politics/features/2008/12/banks200812, accessed on 31 August 2009

Ferguson, Niall (2009a) Diminished returns, *New York Times*, 15 May. Available online at http://www.nytimes.com/2009/05/17/magazine/17wwln-lede-t.html?_r=1, accessed on 20 August 2009

Ferguson, Niall (2009b) The trillion dollar question: China or America? *Daily Telegraph*, 1 June. Available online at http://www.telegraph.co.uk/comment/5424112/The-trillion-dollar-question-China-or-America.html, accessed on 20 August 2009

Ferguson, Niall (2009c) *The ascent of money*, London, Penguin Books

Herbert, Christopher (2002) Filthy lucre: Victorian ideas of money, *Victorian Studies*, winter pp 185-213

Jack, Ian (2008) Money is the strongest taboo in Britain, *Guardian*, 13 December p 35

Kafka, Franz (1974) *The trial* (trans. Muir, Willa and Edwin), Harmondsworth, Penguin

Krugman, Paul (2008) Partying like it's 1929, *New York Times*, 21 March. Available online at http://greatneck.k12.ny.us:16080/GNPS/SMS/departments/social_studies/desiano/documents/1929-NewYorkTimes.pdf, accessed on 21 August 2009

Moss, Stephen and Henley, Jon (2008) Crunch time, *Guardian* G2, 17 September p. 7

McGreal, Chris (2009) Dust to dust for the ghosts of Route 66, *Guardian*, 29 August pp 18-19

Mackay, Charles (1995/1841) *Extraordinary popular delusions and the madness of crowds*, Ware, Herts, Wordsworth Editions

MacMillan, Robert (2008) *Time* Magazine – no depression, 8 October. Available online at http://blogs.reuters.com/mediafile/2008/10/02/time-magazine-no-depression/, accessed on 20 August 2009

Minsky, Hyman (1982) *Inflation, recession and economic policy*, Brighton, Wheatsheaf

National Statistics UK Gross Domestic Product Index. Available online at http://www.statistics.gov.uk/statbase/TSDdownload2.asp, accessed on 13 August 2009

Oldfield, Claire (2009) *The credit crunch commentariat*, London, Editorial Intelligence Ltd. Available online at http://www.editorialintelligence.com/pdf/EI_CreditCrunchCommentariat_Final.pdf, accessed on 13 August 2009

Pearson, Allison (2008) Yes, he's human after all. Allison Pearson gains exclusive access to the Prime Minister, *Daily Mail* 11 October. Available online at http://www.dailymail.co.uk/news/article-1076412/Yes-hes-human-Allison-Pearson-gains-exclusive-access-Prime-Minister.html, accessed on 13 August 2009

Reuters (2008) Ghosts of 1929. Available online at http://www.reuters.com/news/pictures/slideshow?collectionId=2314&galleryName=All%20Collections#a=2, accessed on 20 August 2009

Schacter, Daniel (2001) *The seven sins of memory: How the mind remembers and forgets*, New York, Houghton Mifflin. UK edition 2003, London, Souvenir Press

Schechter, Danny (2009) Credit crisis: How did we miss it?' *British Journalism Review*, Vol.20, No.1, March pp 19-26

Schlicke, Paul (ed.) (1999) *Oxford reader's companion to Dickens*, Oxford, Oxford University Press

Stewart, Heather (2009) Happily, King knows that salvation won't be found in Japan, *Observer* Business and Media, 9 August p. 6

Peter Wilby (2009) Crash Course in Economics, *MediaGuardian*, 27 April 2009 p. 6

Note on Contributor

John Tulloch is Professor of Journalism and Head of the School of Journalism, University of Lincoln. Previously he was chair of the Department of Journalism and Mass Communication at the University of Westminster. Recent work includes jointly editing, with Colin Sparks, *Tabloid tales* (Maryland, Rowman and Littlefield 2000) to which he contributed the essay "The eternal recurrence of the New Journalism". He has written on press regulation, official news management, popular television and the press's coverage of the "war on terror". He has also had a chapter on the journalism of Charles Dickens in *The journalistic imagination: Literary journalists from Defoe to Capote and Carter* (edited by Richard Keeble and Sharon Wheeler; Routledge 2007).

5. Endpiece

Richard Lance Keeble

Ethical Space: At the heart of contemporary communication controversies

Ethical Space is an academic quarterly with a difference. These were the opening words of the journal's first editorial in 2003 and since then its six volumes have certainly lived up to that statement.

In the first instance, the journal, as the voice of the Institute of Communication Ethics (ICE), set itself the distinctly difficult task of drawing together contributions from an eclectic range of disciplines to debate the most important ethical issues of the day. So already represented are philosophy, public relations, health, law, business ethics and corporate social responsibility, education, theology, computing and information studies, research ethics, peace studies, life coaching and counselling, alternative and mainstream journalism (both on and off-line) and politics.

This special double issue of the journal, in focusing on the media coverage of the Great Crash of 2008, is the second in a series of books (jointly edited by John Mair and Richard Lance Keeble) examining contemporary communication controversies through the views of top journalists, PR professionals and academics. The first, published last year (*Beyond trust: Hype and Hope in the British media*), looked at the crucial "trust" issue with lively, opinionated and controversial contributions from a wide variety of experienced and distinguished media practitioners. Peter Wilby, former editor of the *New Statesman* and currently media commentator on the *Guardian*, said of *Beyond trust*: "This collection is excellent on how we got where we are and how commercial imperatives, many of them created in the Thatcher era, changed the way TV in particular operates."

The ICE was launched by Robert Beckett and others in 2001 as an eclectic gathering of academics, researchers, professionals, students and citizens with many different ethical and political perspectives – but all committed to promoting higher standards in the field of communication. As the section headed "Vision" on its website

Richard Lance Keeble (www.communicationethics.net) stresses: "We share a common concern to re-connect with the deeper human values embedded in ethical communication, values held by the institute such as social justice, information integrity, organisational trust, group care and individual well-being."

And it stresses these five main "values":

- independent integrity;
- international network: the editorial board of ES particularly reflects this internationalism – with academics and practitioners drawn from the UK, Spain, Malta, Bosnia, Australia, New Zealand, the US, Holland, Finland, Germany, Hungary, Japan;
- interdisciplinarity;
- practitioner focus;
- caring: significantly, as joint editor, I commented in the introduction to a collection of ES articles (Communication Ethics Now, Troubador 2008): "It is this caring for people – the desperately poor, the inarticulate, the oppressed – along with a sense that honesty, integrity, clarity, respect for difference and diversity are some of the core principles underlying human interaction and, ultimately, communication that drive many of the writings in Ethical Space."

Ethical stance defined clearly – but broadly

In an editorial in Vol. 3, Nos 2 and 3 of 2006, the joint editor, Dr Donald Matheson, of Canterbury University, New Zealand, stressed that ethics could be defined narrowly, as a matter of duty or responsibility. Or ethics could be defined broadly "blurring into areas such as politics and social criticism". *Ethical Space* stood essentially at the blurred end of the definitional range. He continued: "As many commentators have pointed out, a discussion of ethics that is divorced from politics is immediately unable to talk about some of the most important factors in shaping communication and media practices."

There are already a number of excellent journals providing scholarly critiques of communication ethics. For instance, there's the *Journal of Applied Ethics*, the *Journal of Mass Media Ethics* and the *Journal of Information, Communication and Ethics in Society*. *Ethical Space* has particularly close links with the Boston-based *Media Ethics* journal edited by John Michael Kittross (see http://www.mediaethicsmagazine.com/).

But while these journals continue to plug away at their central priorities, *Ethical Space* occupies its unique, interdisciplinary place – believing that ethics needs to be made relevant "through its collision with a range of ways of producing knowledge about communication". As Cees J. Hamelink, Professor Emeritus of the University of Amsterdam, has pointed out: "Moral questions are often couched in terms of dilemmas for which solutions must be found from deontological, utilitarian or discursive methodologies. The solutions are unusually ambiguous and unsatisfactory. Ethical inquiry needs to be more creative and deconstruct situations that look like dilemmas into configurations of a wide variety of moral options and challenges. That is why we are very fortunate to have such important platforms as *Ethical Space* for this exercise in new forms of reflection!"

Unique range of genres
Ethical Space is also unique in the ways in which it carries contributions in a range of genres:

- news items feature at the start of every issue. The news section also provides a space in which ICE's activities (such as annual conferences and workshops) and publications can be publicised;
- "views" are lively, often controversial and always topical "think pieces" of around 1,500-2,000 words;
- "articles" are more substantial pieces, referenced, of around 3,000 words;
- "face to face" interviews – conducted by blogger and media commentator Kristine Lowe;
- "papers" are 5,000-word academic pieces (all rigorously peer reviewed) which form the intellectual backbone of the journal;
- the journal usually ends (conventionally) with reviews of books and websites.

Journalism at the heart of *ES*
Given the preoccupation of the joint editors, it is perhaps not surprising that journalism is the discipline at the heart of ICE's activities. And both practitioners and academics have made important contributions to *ES* debates. For instance, Roy Greenslade, *Guardian* blogger and Professor of Journalism at City University, London, asked: "Does ethical journalism inevitably mean dull journalism?" Nicholas Jones, for 30 years a BBC political and industrial correspondent, argued that there was a "window of opportunity" to change the way the government communicated with the media following the Hutton Inquiry into the death of weapons inspector Dr David Kelly; Michael Foley, top Dublin journalist and head of journalism at the Dublin Institute of Technology, explored the complex issues surrounding the use of confidential sources by reporters while broadcaster, *Times* columnist and novelist Libby Purves wondered why ethical

Richard Lance Keeble

idealism faded with age.

Professor Clifford Christians, of the University of Illinois-Urbana, said by many to be the world's leading authority on communication ethics with a host of publications (such as *Media Ethics: Cases and Moral Reasoning*) and academic honours to his name, has been a prominent supporter of ICE since its launch. And he has made a number of important contributions to *Ethical Space*, helping to identify its underlying philosophy and aims. For instance, in a seminal paper entitled "The media and moral literacy", he argued: "Our social existence is conjoined linguistically and because the lingual is not neutral but value-laden, social bonds are moral claims. Therefore, given that our public life is not merely functional but knit together by social values, the various technologies of public communication should engender moral literacy."

More academic studies of journalism have included Angelika W. Wyka, a PhD candidate at the Frankfurt Graduate School, Germany, examining journalistic standards and democratisation of the mass media in Poland, Hungary and the Czech Republic, Professor John Tulloch, of the University of Lincoln, looking at the British press's coverage of torture and the human rights of terrorist suspects, and Professor Chris Atton, of Napier University, Edinburgh, exploring ethical issues in alternative journalism.

A number of *ES* issues have been guest-edited. This has helped expand the range of contributors and perspectives in the journal and allowed for the publication of the proceedings of important (yet otherwise ignored) conferences and workshops. For instance, Dr Martin Conboy, of Sheffield University, chaired a seminar at the 9th conference of the International Society for the Study of European Ideas at the University of Navarro, Pamplona, entitled "Popular ethics in journalism: Individual burden or collective responsibility". And the talks at that seminar were drawn together in a special "Pamplona Papers" issue (Vol. 2, No. 1).

In his editorial, Dr Conboy made this important point: "Ethical journalism can only be developed through a dialogic engagement between individual responsibility (of journalist, educator and reader) and the collective burden of institutions and social and political groupings. It also needs to define itself within or against the prevailing pragmatics of the market. Such journalism needs to be popular in the broadest sense of the word for it to provide a suitably critical model for intervention in the contemporary world." His own contribution to the seminar focused on the radical journalism of Thomas Wooler's *Black Dwarf* (1817-24), highlighting its carnivalesque mix of parody, satire and libertarian rhetoric which both exposed the limitations of journalism fixed within a capitalist system but also offered a more radical and popular engagement through its textual experimentation.

Another area of particular interest: PR
Another field of particular interest to *Ethical Space* is PR ethics. Anne Gregory, the UK's only full-time Professor of Public Relations, of Leeds Metropolitan University, has been closely involved in ICE's activities from the start and has contributed a number of important papers to the journal: for instance, on government communications and on the public relations of a large Mental Health NHS Trust. Simon Goldsworthy, Senior Lecturer in PR at the University of Westminster, has also appeared regularly at ICE conferences and contributed (often witty) pieces and reviews to *ES*. In a piece entitled: "PR ethics: Forever a will o' the wisp", he wrote: "Nourished by the understandable desire of a commonly derided industry to prove itself respectable, plenty of lush moralistic vegetation flourishes. Indeed, well-known PR educators have described the role of PR as one of promoting 'loving' relations, and given the impression that 'Nelson Mandela and Mother Theresa [sic] would have struggled to qualify for admittance to the Institute for Public Relations'."

ICE has developed close links with a number of UK and international organisations and this is reflected in the contents of *Ethical Space*. One of them is the Radical PR group, and the proceedings from their conference in Stirling during the autumn of 2008 formed a special issue (Vol 6, No.2), guest edited by Johanna Fawkes, former Principal Lecturer at Leeds Metropolitan University. In her own paper, Johanna Fawkes argued that professional ethics could benefit from considering the ideas of Carl Jung (1875) regarding wholeness instead of goodness as the goal of the integrated psyche. "The whole self then becomes the basis for ethics in contrast to the ideal-typical self at the heart of many approaches to professional ethics."

Guest edited issues – extending the focus
Another special issue (Vol. 3, No. 40 of 2006), guest edited by Professor Gavin Fairbairn, of Leeds Metropolitan University, focused on health, care and communication ethics. Between them, the papers covered a wide range of highly complex issues including the nature of ethical communication between doctors and their clients and the challenges facing professionals who care for dying children – such as truth telling, informed consent and the right of dying children to receive spiritual care. For those particularly interested in communication ethics and the internet, a special issue (Vol. 4, Nos 1 and 1, 2007), edited by Dr Matheson, was devoted to this subject.

ICE annual conferences have also provided a rich source of copy for *Ethical Space*. The 2005 conference explored the impact of communication ethical theory on teaching practice. Raphael Cohen-

Almagor, Professor in Politics at the University of Hull, examined the concept of compromise through a discussion of teaching about abortion – drawing on his personal experience of running a series of seminars on this subject in the US. John Strain, director of the Centre for Applied and Professional Ethics at the University of Surrey, in a paper entitled "The importance of caring: Ethics, communication and higher education", highlighted the importance of communication in the ethics of all professions and identified the scope for collaboration across the different professions, while Brian Hoey, of Northumbria University, identified ways in which arts tutors could use life coaching to enhance their skills.

The 2008 annual conference, boldly titled "Whistleblowers and mischief-makers: The ethics of scandal" proved a terrific success: the range of issues covered – from the politics of sleaze coverage by top investigative reporter Tessa Mayes, to the psychological origins of scapegoating by Professor Karen Sanders – was utterly fascinating. Particularly pleasing was the presence of students who sat attentively alongside communication professionals and academics and engaged in the "café" discussions. Indeed, the work of excellent postgraduate students (such as Florian Zollmann, Angelika Wyka and Dean Ritz) has been an important feature of *ES*.

Alan Lane, of VASGAMA, argued that PR practitioners had to face a harsh new reality: no longer could they claim innocence of corporate corruption. They were now as accountable as any chief executive for any wrongdoings. And Michael Ford, a BBC ethics specialist, argued that journalists needed to be more aware of the psychological subtleties of a person's sexuality when covering gay stories.

Success for *Ethical Space*

This overview has given only a brief idea of the rich miscellany of articles which have made up *Ethical Space* to date. But during its brief life, it has already recorded some notable successes. Volume 1 appeared in book form as *Communication Ethics Today* (Troubador, 2005) while Volume 2 was called *Communication Ethics Now* (Troubador, 2008). Plans are under-way to have Volumes 3-6 published by Arima of Bury St. Edmunds.

The results from the UK's research assessment exercise suggest that ES articles submitted were ranked of "high international status" while the journal was recently given an "A" ranking in Australia's equivalent of the RAE. Moreover, recent figures suggest that ICE's website (www.communicationethics.net where a selection of *ES* articles is accessible free) receives up to 72,000 hits a month. So its message is clearly getting heard!

Note on Contributor

Richard Lance Keeble has edited *Ethical Space* since its launch. He is the author and editor of 14 books including *The newspapers handbook* (Routledge, fourth edition 2005); *Ethics for journalists* (Routledge, second edition, 2008); *Secret state, silent press: New militarism, the Gulf and the modern image of warfare* (John Libbey, 1997) and with Sharon Wheeler, *The journalistic imagination: Literary journalists from Defoe to Capote and Carter* (Routledge, 2007). His books have been translated into a number of languages including Chinese, Romanian and Ukrainian. His research interests include the links between mainstream journalists and the intelligence services and the journalism of George Orwell. He is currently co-editing a book on peace journalism and writing a history of war reporting from 1945. Since 2003, he has been Professor of Journalism at the University of Lincoln.

Ethical Space Book No. 2

Communication Ethics Now, drawing together articles from Volume 2 (2005) of *Ethical Space: The International Journal of Communication Ethics*, has just been published. In a foreword, Cees Hamelink, professor emeritus of International Communication at the University of Amsterdam, comments: "Ethical inquiry needs to be more creative and deconstruct situations that look like dilemmas into configurations of a wide variety of moral options and challenges. We are very fortunate to have such important platforms as *Communication Ethics Now* for this exercise in new forms of reflection!"

He adds: "This book convincingly demonstrates how lively and relevant today's ethical reflections on communication can be. The chapters of the book cover such an exciting and broad range of topics."

Edited by Richard Keeble, joint editor of Ethical Space, the 25 chapters are divided into five sections. In the first, which focuses on journalism ethics, John Tulloch examines the British press's coverage of the CIA torture flights (better known as "extraordinary rendition") while Julie-ann Davies reports on the media's increasing use of anonymous sources. Jane Taylor takes a particularly unusual look at the media's obsession with celebrity focusing on the coverage of Carole Chaplin, Cherie Blair's "style guru" and broadcaster, novelist and columnist Libby Purves expresses outrage at the media's daily diet of "unkind intrusions and falsifications".

In an international section, leading Nigerian academic Kate Azuka Omenugha explores the representation of Africanness in the British press, Susanne Fengler and Stephan Russ-Mohl express concern over the slump in media standards in Germany while Angelika W. Wyka focuses on journalistic standards and democratization of the mass media in Poland, Hungary and the Czech Republic.

In a section that takes a historical perspective on journalism ethics, Jane Chapman's chapter looks at "Republican Citizenship, Ethics and the French Revolutionary Press 1789-92" while Martin Conboy's focuses on Wooler's *Black Dwarf*, a radical journal of the early 19th century.

Another section on communication ethics and pedagogy draws on papers at the 2005 annual conference of the Institute of Communication Ethics with contributions from Raphael Cohen-Almagor, John Strain, Brian Hoey, Brian Morris, Simon Goldsworthy and Anne Gregory. The philosophical dimensions of communication ethics are explored by Karen Sanders, Hallvard Johannes Fossheim (in an interview with Kristine Lowe) Robert Beckett, Moira Carroll-Mayer and Bernd Carsten Stahl. In the final section on business and communication ethics, Kristine Lowe interviews Paul Jackson, of Manchester Business School.

- *Communication Ethics Now* is published by Troubador, Leicester, for £12.99 For more details see: http://www.troubador.co.uk/book_info.asp?bookid=623. It follows the success of *Communication Ethics Today*, also published by Troubador, which drew on articles in the first volume of Ethical Space. See http://www.troubador.co.uk/book_info.asp?bookid=296

Trust under the spotlight in new ICE book

2007-2008 was the *annus horribilis* for the British media. All terrestrial broadcasters were found to have cheated their audiences through a variety of scams: Premium Rate Calling, fake competitions with results changed to suit the producers – and more. As a result, public trust in the media dipped.

Beyond Trust: Hype and hope in the British media, published by the Institute of Communication Ethics, examines this crucial 'trust' issue with lively, opinionated and controversial contributions from a wide variety of experienced and distinguished media practitioners. It places the contemporary controversy in a historical context, examines the implications for local newspapers – and explores the role media education can play in restoring trust. In addition:

- Anthony Arblaster, former *Tribune* journalist, argues the case for scepticism
- Dorothy Byrne, head of News and Current Affairs at Channel Four, claims: 'TV journalism is so fair it makes Andy Pandy look dodgy'
- Charlie Beckett, director of Polis@LSE, asks: 'Can we trust the internet?'
- Suzanne Franks, director of research at the Centre for Journalism, University of Kent, assesses the BBC's performances in covering the Second World War and the 'Troubles' in Ireland
- Richard Peel, director of corporate affairs for Camelot, explores critically the often tense relationships between PROs and journalists
- John Tulloch, professor of journalism at the University of Lincoln, presents a wide-ranging overview of the trust debate in a controversial Afterword.

Beyond trust (ISBN 978 1 84549 341 7) is edited by John Mair, senior lecturer in journalism at Coventry University and a former producer and director for BBC, ITV and Channel Four, and Richard Lance Keeble, professor of journalism at the University of Lincoln and joint editor of *Ethical Space: The International Journal of Communication Ethics*. It is published by Arima Publishing, of Bury St Edmunds (www.abramis.co.uk; £14.95)

The Institute of Communication Ethics

ICE aims to:

- formalise the study and practice in the fast growing discipline of CE and articulate the communication industries' concerns with ethical reasoning and outcomes;

- provide communication practitioners with a centre to drive the study of ethical practice in communications;

- develop specific tools, quality frameworks and training methods and provide them to its members; assess initiatives in related disciplines and offer guidance and ethics training for communicators;

- offer qualifications that support the practice of communication as an ethical discipline underpinned by principles, rules of conduct and systematic self-examination.

Membership Application

I would like to apply for annual membership to the ICE with:

☐ Personal membership with access to *Ethical Space* online (£55)
☐ Personal membership plus printed copy of *Ethical Space* (£75)
☐ Organisational membership (non profit £200, for profit (small) £500, multinational £5000)

Note: Please contact the ICE office for further details of local chapters of ICE.

Name _____

Address _____

_____

Country _____ Postcode _____

Email _____

Tel _____ Fax _____

Name of University/Institute/Organisation _____

_____

Payment

☐ I enclose a cheque payable to 'Institute of Communication Ethics'

Please return to: ICE, Faculty of Media, Business and Marketing, Leeds Trinity and All Saints, Brownberrie Lane, Horsforth, Leeds LS18 5HD, UK.

For assistance please contact: info@communication-ethics.net

www.ingramcontent.com/pod-product-compliance
Lightning Source LLC
Chambersburg PA
CBHW080444110426
42743CB00016B/3275